TEX SMITH'S
Hot Rod
LIBRARY

HOW TO BUILD
FAT
FORDS
1935-1948

By Rich Johnson

First published in 1991 by Motorbooks International Publishers & Wholesalers, PO Box 2, 729 Prospect Avenue, Osceola, WI 54020 USA

Created by Tex Smith Publishing Co. PO Box 726, 29 East Wallace, Driggs, ID 83422

Library of Congress Cataloging-in-Publication Data

How to build fat Fords / by Rich Johnson
   p.   cm.
ISBN 0-87938-479-4
   1. Ford automobile--Customizing. I. Hot rod mechanix
TL215.3.F7H627   1991
629.28 ' 722—dc20   90-37744
                                                CIP

Printed and bound in the United States of America

CONTENTS

Publisher	LEROI TEX SMITH
Editor	RICHARD JOHNSON
Tech. Editor	RON CERIDONO
Art Director	BOB REECE
Art Assistant	VICKY DAVIDSON
Copy Editor	BECKY JAYE
Circulation	JANET SMITH

FOREWORD
Deja Vu...Again

Somehow, I think we've been here before. Fat Fords, I mean. It is all the current rage to preach about how the entire hot rod hobby is running downhill overdrive into Fat Fords. Those cars built between 1935 and 1948. By implication, I suppose, that means that all Fords built prior to 1935 would be Skinny Fords. Certainly, those fatter than rotund Fords and Mercurys built from 1949 through 1954 would seem to be Ultra Fat. But not so. They are Shoeboxes. To be sure, anyone who wants to practice hot rodding on an intimate basis must indeed learn a completely new vernacular.

Interestingly, the term Fat Fords (and derivative spin-offs such as Fat's Where It's At, Fat Attack, etc.) were not a part of general hot rodding lingo until perhaps a decade ago. At the same time, 1935 and later Fords were not particularly popular in the hobby of street rodding a decade ago. Which I find perplexing. Because way back in the "olden times" of rodding, the fats were everywhere, often much more popular than A-bones and Deuces.

Not so many years ago, there was a general consensus among rod and custom enthusiasts that 1935 and later Fords were Customs that were sometimes Hot Rods. The reasoning was that these were 1) New cars, and 2) Round cars that didn't look good without fenders. The real icing was that these cars looked good with fender skirts, which was at the time the absolute criteria for a custom car.

Still, there were some rodders who tended to ignore such edicts. They would build the New and Round cars, paying special attention to the engine/transmission/rearend so that the result was a very fast New and Round car. Sometimes such hot rods would have the rear springs heated (lowered the car, but not as much as a tail dragging custom), but usually these cars relied on big rear tires and slightly smaller front tires for a "rubber rake." A hot rodded fat Ford was never confused with a customized fat Ford, but on occasion a customized fat Ford was also given a full engine treatment. Well up into the 1950s, it wasn't uncommon to see a customized fat Ford running at southern California's dry lakes, or even at a drag strip. But, it was far more common to see a hot rodded fat Ford at competition events. Both were considered part and parcel of hot rodding.

However, within the framework of what could be called a fat Ford, there were some definite "yes" and "no" projects. A 1935 was almost always converted to a 1936 (hood and grille swap). A 1939 Standard almost always became at least a 1939 Deluxe (hood and grille swap), and sometimes it would become a 1940 Deluxe. On rare occasion a 1941 would get a 1946-'48 hood and grille (which always led to an interesting side chrome mismatch), and the 1946 could be counted on to get trim/grille (sometimes front fenders) from a 1948. You'll notice there is no mention of the 1937 and 1938 Fords. Because back in the olden times, we considered them ugly beyond redemption!

Yes, there were a few pockets of avant garde, such as the Pacific Northwest, where these cars were rodded or customized. Dig back through issues of Hot Rod magazine, or any of the pocket-book size magazines, and you'll find a rare '37/'38. Even then, however, those cars really didn't look all that bad (as viewed with our less-prejudiced eyes of today).

But what really started making the fat Fords into today's Fat Fords (with a few really FAT FORDS thrown in), was the trick of getting the bodies down in the weeds. Cement scrapers. Street huggers. Even this practice gives a front tire to fender relationship that would not have been acceptable design as little as 15 years ago. Now, if big rear tires can be tucked inside the rear fenders, great. If tiny little fronts can be bolted in place, all the better. It is a kind of drag racer comic car look that has been made more than acceptable by drag racing pro-stocks, and magazine cartoonists.

Add to this the practice of painting much of the original bright work (particularly the grille), and you end up with a rotund lump that's most pleasing. This one-ness type of painting has tended to blend the individual shapes into a single bulbous object that can, in itself, accent the hot rod theme. Designers have been quick to seize on this thread.

Twenty or thirty years ago, starting in about 1960, a traditional hot rodder (meaning someone who builds pre-1935 cars) would often have a fat Ford on the premises. But there was always an asterisk after the fact: "I bought it for my wife!" Yeah, sure. But the fat thing turned out to be a great work car, a kind of daily driver. Remember, in 1960, a 1946 Ford was only 14 years old. A great used car. But, it was always relegated to being left home when some "real" hot rod-

ding was to be done. Yes, there were a few exceptions, but those were the really brave hot rodders, the people we now realize were true hot rodders from the very beginning.

The neat thing about building a fat Ford, or even a FAT FORD, is that you can do whatever you want. You can make up a near stocker, with a stock engine/ driveline. Nobody puts you down. You can swap a late model suspension, whack the top, section the body, bolt on a dozen superchargers. Nobody puts you down. It may not always be this liberal, which is only important if you care especially about what someone else thinks about your car. But for now, there are no building restraints on fat Fords. Do it the way you wanna. Use it the way you wanna. Even the restoration purists tend to accept hot rodded fat Fords.

And there is a ready supply of material from which to build. Sure, the pre-WWII cars are getting scarce, but 1946-'48 Fords and Mercurys (and even a few Lincolns) are in good supply. Strangely enough, the 4-door sedans are rarest of all, which means that when such a lowly body style is built today, it gets extra attention. But, as with all older cars, trying to find converts is really searching for the needle. Because of this, some builders are using the decent top portions of converts (cars that have rusted away below the belt line) and adapting the pieces to more common coupes. We have talked with a couple of convert owners (1941-'48 types) who did not have top bows, and they have found that the folding tops from compact cars of the 1960s can be made to fit. All this means that the fat cars may offer more parts interchangeability than the older Fords ever had. A very nice state of affairs for the home builder on a budget.

Much of what you see in this book is aimed at the home craftsman, the person who does most of his/ her own work, using junkyard parts, and an occasional mail-order specialty item. But more and more hot rod and custom car aftermarket suppliers are building items for the fat Fords. Advertising in this book attests to that fact. This will make it easier and easier to create a fat attack of your own. Even complete frames will come on line (in addition to what is already out there), and a total line of fiberglass bodies is assured. The fat Fords of tomorrow will be where the A's and Deuces are today.

The bottom line to all this is that fat Fords are not new. Neither are FAT FORDS. They are just becoming more common. Again. I like that. I think you must, also, else why would you be reading this book?

LeRoi Tex Smith
Publisher

WHAT TO BUILD

by LeRoi Tex Smith

Fat, as in rotund. Round. Heavy duty. Strangely, this is a term for the later model hot rod Fords that was never considered a couple of decades ago. During the 1940s and 1950s, these cars were simply considered "new" versus the "used" Model T's and Model A's and early V8s.

Early on, there was a distinction between a "hot rod" and a "custom." Generally, any car sporting skirts was a custom, and it wasn't until the 1935 Ford design that fender skirts seemed to really fit. That was when the pontoon fenders began to appear in earnest. Cars began to take on a rounder appearance. They seemed more sleek, more tuned into streamlining and highway cruising. They didn't look very good with the fenders removed.

So it was back in the olden day that 1935 and newer Fords were usually customized more than they were hot rodded. Oh, they got plenty of hopped-up flathead V8 engines, and they could usually hold their own with the lighter weight A-V8s. But it remained for the ohv-V8 engine swap craze of the '50s to really make these "new" Fords popular.

First, the 1939 and 1940 coupes took off, then the 1936 coupes, both 3-window and 5-window versions, enjoyed a surge of interest. Finally, the 1941 and later business coupes got the nod. As customs as well as hot rods. During this time, the 1939 and later Mercs had a sparse following, and the Lincoln Zephyr even fewer devotees. But all that is nostalgia now. Because today, you can build a fat Ford just about any way you want to.

Still, there are some restraints and considerations. For instance, a 1935 Ford is a relatively small car inside where comfort counts. Because the '35 and '36 models have been popular with restorers for the past two decades, good versions are sometimes hard to find at bargain

The great thing about fat Fords is that you can still find good buildable projects lurking in junkyards and farmsteads, even in the middle of larger towns.

At one time, not many years ago, no one wanted to build a 1935 rod or custom, but now they are all the rage. The 2-door is more popular than the 4-door.

basement prices. Certainly, finding a great condition car out in some farmyard is very rare indeed. For this reason, anyone contemplating building a 1935-'36 Ford of any body style may want to first consider trying to find a restored version. Prices on these once high-dollar restorations have plummeted in recent years, as the early Ford V8 craze has died. It is quite possible to pick up a good body style coupe or Tudor for as little as $5000. Convertibles and roadsters, being rare, still demand more cash. The advantage of buying a restoration is obvious: You get a car with most of the cosmetics already done. You can then scrounge up a spare frame, create the hot rod or custom chassis you want, and swap over the body.

Keeping a car original in body appearance was once a popular thing to do, but in the last ten years modified cars have appreciated in sales price so much that the resto-rod phase has passed from street rodding. Whether or not it will return is unknown. But, if you want to go ahead and modify the restored body, it is a matter of personal taste.

At the same time, there are now some really great early fat Ford fiberglass bodies available. The 1935-'36 is marketed as a convert or roadster, even the "ugly duckling" 1937-'38 converts are finding ready buyers. These bodies are slightly higher than the older Fords, but they also require more materials and engineering. Gene Winfield is even making a fiberglass 1946-'48 coupe, available with the top chopped, a basic body that is widely accepted as state of the art.

The 1937-'38 Fords, in all but the open body styles, were once considered too ugly to build. No longer is that the case, but finding a convertible or sedan convertible from those years is almost impossible. For this reason, many builders are making "phantom" '37-'38 Fords. They are cutting the top from coupes and sedans, usually fitting a padded convert type top, or running no top at all. These cars are rather widely available, since they escaped the first onslaught of hot rodders and restorers.

The 1939-'40 Fords, all body styles, have always been popular as restorations, rods and customs. The 4-door sedans were never as desirable as the 2-doors, so this body style went to the dumps early on. Nowadays, finding a good 4-door is hard, and they always generate lots of interest at rod runs. But, since they are a 4-door, they also command the lowest dollar when you are dickering to buy. It is a toss-up whether to go with a '39 or '40 front end, but the '40 Deluxe is still considered the epitome of style for these cars.

The 1939 and 1940 Mercury is different from the Ford in many ways, and finding one suitable for building is quite difficult. Same with the Lincolns.

The 1941 Ford/Merc body style is the beginning of the Box Fat, if such a term can be employed. These are the really fat Fords, in a kind of square way. They are not streamlined, and they are not swoopy, unless the

Almost as rare as a roadster or convertible is the 3-window '35-'36 coupe. These have always been popular with rodders.

The 5-window '35-'36 coupe (this is a '36) uses a more common production line body style, still these early coupes are hard to find.

This '36 coupe has been sectioned. Note height of hood to fender. These first-of-the-fats were once considered more as customs than as rods.

tops are chopped and fender fadeaways are used.

The 1941 seems to be the same as the later 1946-'48 models, but it is different in several ways. The big difference is the front sheetmetal and grille(s), but there is a belt line fold in the metal that also sets the car apart. It is also slightly different in frame measurements, being more like the 1940.

The 1946-'48 Fords/Mercs are one of a feather. Only minor changes were made in trim and mechanicals on these cars (the Mercury is longer), so there is a tremendous amount of interchangeability. And, these cars seem to still be everywhere in America and Canada. Of all the fat Fords, the 1946-'48 models are the most plentiful, and the least costly (except special woodies and convertibles). The 2-door models were very common then, and still are, perhaps more of them being available today than 4-door versions. Gerry Charvat, a Fort Wayne pro builder, has found it possible to locate cars of this era in good body condition. He buys a western states car, with little or no rust, and can often get one so reasonable that even after he does a Chevelle frame swap, a turn-key car can be built for under $5000! That is incredible, and one reason that anyone contemplating a fat Ford should look very strongly at a 1941-'48 model.

These cars are very roomy inside, feature couch-height seating, and excellent visibility. A kind of plus to such a car is that there is good visibility to the front and sides (sight out the rear window is poor on all fat Fords). Even when the car has been slammed to the pavement (discounting a top chop), the cars are favorites with women who must drive in heavy traffic.

All fat Fords are definitely a giant step up from the Model A type of hot rod. These are comfort cars, but they can still be performance monsters. Overall weight difference between a 1948 Ford coupe and a 1934 Ford coupe is just a couple hundred pounds. Weight distribution is slightly different, with the fat Ford having the engine move forward over the axle centerline as the years progress.

As a general rule, the later model fat Ford you select, the easier it will be to get basic building projects, and parts. It is also less expensive to build the later models. A variation to this rule will be the wood bodied Sportsman converts (extremely rare) and woodie wagons.

Another rule of thumb is that the older the car, the more work will be required to bring it back to life. Mostly because of rust damage and years of torture. So, if you are not heavy into building, you'll want to stay with the later models, perhaps using the 1939 as the oldest version to consider.

Ultimately, however, whatever fat Ford you build, you're gonna like the results. They ride nice, they handle well, and with modern power, they are both economical and practical.

The 1937-'38 Fords have never been as popular as now. This photo was taken in the mid-Fifties, we use it to prove that fat Fords have always been a part of rodding.

Starting in 1938, the Standard model used "last year's" grille treatment. The Deluxe version had an updated grille. In this lineup there are '38 Standard and Deluxe, '39 Standard and Deluxe, and '40 Standard and Deluxe.

The woodie wagon was a part of all fat Ford years. This 1940 Deluxe version is a pure resto-rod style.

The 1939 Deluxe and 1940 Standard look almost identical. The difference is minor trim changes.

Fat Ford pickups have always been popular. The 1937 and '38 versions were least appreciated of all. In 1940, the Standard or Deluxe grille could be used.

When looking for a fat Ford project, don't overlook what would be an earlier attempt at customizing. This Mercury sports special may seem ungainly, but it would make a great resurrection.

The 1941 Mercury featured side "wing" grilles. There is a similarity to the 1941 Ford. Woodies are hard to find and expensive to rebuild.

The 1941 Mercury had a chevron grille, while the 1941 Ford used a 3-piece grille. The '41 Ford also has slightly different body lines down the belt line area from later Fords.

Fat Fords include business and 5-passenger coupes, as well as convertibles. This is the long model convertible, 1948 version. 1946 Ford has short pieces of horizontal chrome trim off the trunk handle, and grooved side trim.

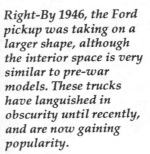

Right-By 1946, the Ford pickup was taking on a larger shape, although the interior space is very similar to pre-war models. These trucks have languished in obscurity until recently, and are now gaining popularity.

1947-'48 Fords use fat side trim. The difference between the two is placement of the parking lights and a piece of chrome trim atop each front fender.

Right-The Lincoln, introduced as a Zephyr model in 1937 (very sleek), grew boxy with the Continental styling in 1939-'48. These cars are rare, but enough have been rodded to make them sort of top-of-the-line.

FAT FORD ID GUIDE

by John Lee

Annual styling changes were already a way of life at Ford Motor Company by the mid-1930s. Just enough changes were made each year to make it obvious to the neighbors that you were driving last year's car, not the current model.

One body shell was usually used for two or three years with yearly modifications of easily changed items like the grille, trim and taillights to give it a new look.

The Model T debuted in 1909 and continued

in production for almost 20 years with changes and improvements incorporated as they were developed. The 1929 Model A was little changed from the 1928, but 1930 brought a new grille and fenders, and another radiator grille shell change distinguished the '31.

1932 was an unusual one-model year, one of the factors that's kept it at the top of the hot rodders' wish list for so long. It was a transitional model between the A and the Model 40, which covered the years 1933 and 1934, with only moderate change between the two, most evident in the hood louver and grille shapes.

1935 began a period of rapid change from the square styles of the 1920s to the finned, aircraft style designs of the 1950s. The era of the fat fendered Fords would see running boards disappear, fenders blend into the body, grilles evolve from fancy radiator covers to an integral and identifying feature of the package.

All these 1935-'48 fat fenders are more than 40 years old by now, and many of them have been altered over the years. A review is in order to refresh the memories of those who grew up with these models, and maybe educate some younger enthusiasts about the differences that will help you identify them correctly.

1935 models were becoming rounded. Grille was V'd but rolled under at the bottom, rather than ending in a point like the '34s.

Top right-Most Fords for '35 had a built-in trunk. Taillights were still on stands, and there was still a slightly concave sweep to the fenders. Phil Wright of the Briggs Body Company is credited with the design.

The Colorado Courtesy Patrol drove silver and black 1935 Ford 2-door coaches.

Fenders of the '36 have a more convex rearward sweep than the '35. Hood side louvers have three trim strips instead of four.

Bob Koto performed the facelift for the 1936 models. Grille has a sharper Vee with horizontal bars eliminated.

Separate windshield posts and no windows in the doors distinguish the '36 roadster, an all-time favorite with rodders, customizers and restorers.

The '35 cabriolet has roll-up windows. This one also has a rumble seat, as indicated by the handle to open it from the top.

Both a phaeton (no roll-up windows) and a 4-door convertible sedan, like the one pictured, were still offered for 1936.

The 1937 Ford took its styling cues, especially the sharp "prow" grille, from the new Lincoln Zephyr. Windshield was V'd for the first time.

Rear of the '37 coupe is similar to the '36. Fenders blend into a gravel shield below the deck lid. Both 85-horsepower and economy 60-horsepower flathead V8s were offered.

In 1938, Ford started a new practice of carrying over the previous year's styling, slightly modified, for the Standard series and presenting new style in the Deluxe series. This is a '38 Standard coupe.

The '38 Deluxe coupe had a new grille, still featuring horizontal bars, but with the hood extending into a Vee to divide it into right and left halves. Hood louvers continue the grille's horizontal line theme. Headlights on this one have been converted to sealed beams.

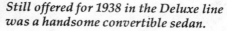

Still offered for 1938 in the Deluxe line was a handsome convertible sedan.

14

15

1939 Standard coupe had much the same look as the '38 Deluxe. Bright bars divide the grille into sections, and "bullet" hood side relief extends forward to cut the top bars shorter. Hood side louvers are also shorter. Teardrop headlights are similar to '37.

Above-A convertible sedan in the 1939 Deluxe lineup makes a beautiful street rod. Teardrop headlights were moved out onto the fenders, and lower Vee grille features vertical bars.

Right-Teardrop taillights of the '39 Ford were destined to become hot rodding classics. Convertible sedan deck is now rounded like the sedan.

Above-New for 1940 headlight design has parking light lens in the top of the bright rim, and sealed beam lenses. Lights designate this Standard sedan as a '40, although grille is nearly the same as '39 Deluxe.

Right - It is not uncommon to see '39 Fords masquerading as '40 models. Although this car sports '40 headlights, an identification key is the position of the windshield wipers. In '40, the wipers were relocated below the glass. Other differences are the dashboard and the fact that '39 windshields cranked out.

A '40 Deluxe coupe in black with flames over the hood and front fenders says hot rod as loud as any model. Deluxe grille is divided into four sections.

Above-For 1941, Ford brought out its new rounded bodies that would remain in production through 1948, although interrupted for nearly four years by World War II. Sealed beam headlights are set wide in the fenders, and running boards are partially concealed by body flairs.

Left-Super Deluxe was a new top-trim series for 1941, identified by chrome plating of all three grille sections. Bright trim tracing fender character lines was added at mid-year. This convertible's hood is welded into one piece and nosed, with the beltline strip shortened — strictly '50s style!

Above-New taillights on the '41s were vertical rectangles. The business coupe (shown) has shorter doors and larger quarter windows than the club coupe.

Left-The biggest change for '42 was the grille, which was wider and made up of curved vertical bars with only a narrow center piece retaining the 3-section theme from 1941. This one was treated to '55 Cadillac headlight doors and a shaved and louvered hood.

The '42 model adopted the horizontal oval taillights which would also be continued through 1948. Deluxe bumpers were the same as '41 Super Deluxe. Running boards were fully concealed.

"Hash marks" were removed from the '46 top grille bar and the grooves were absent from the horizontal grille bars on the '47 models. Parking lights remained rectangular horizontal units placed inboard of the headlights, but some sources say Ford switched to 1948 round style during the year.

The first models out after the war were changed little. Grille now consisted of horizontal bars, rather than vertical, though parking light placement was the same as '42. Super Deluxe models had bright moldings around the windows.

Taillights were still the same horizontal oval units for 1947.

The horizontal bars of the '46 Ford grille had indentations painted with a red stripe and six vertical indentations in the chrome top bar. The sedan delivery had Deluxe trim.

The 1948 models had round parking lights below the headlights, smooth bumpers with guards of a new design, and bolder fender moldings placed slightly below the character lines rather than above them as previously.

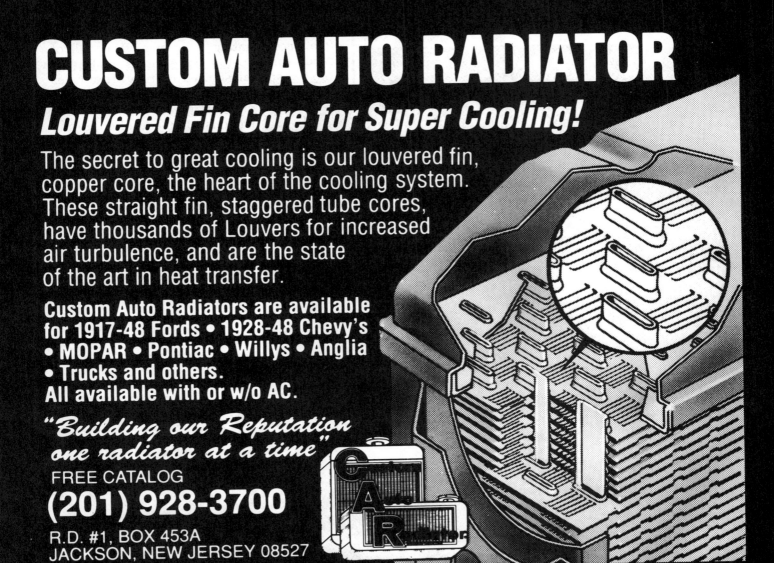

FAT CUSTOMS

by John Lee

Having been among the most popular cars for rodding and restyling over the years, Fords from the fat era have undergone every conceivable body and mechanical alteration.

Harry Westergard is often credited with starting the fat customizing craze with his LaSalle-grilled '36. The Ayala brothers and the Barris brothers torched a good number of these models before FoMoCo brought out the shoebox Fords and the bathtub Mercs for them to work on.

Backyard builders across the country reworked many more, sometimes copying what they'd seen in a magazine or at a show or, more often, incorporating their own ideas. All of Trend's early <u>Custom Car Annuals</u> and <u>Restyle Your Car</u> specials showed a variety of examples from this era, some of which were quite imaginative, others rather hideous. The plentiful, cheap and relatively lively Ford V8 chassis and running gear formed the basis of innumerable backyard sports specials.

On the following pages, we present a few customizing ideas that have been used over the years. Maybe they'll stimulate your imagination and desire to create an original look for your fat fendered Ford.

A top chop and filled hood side panels look great on a 1936 Ford 3-window coupe.

This is not a production '37 pickup, rather a custom concoction that mates a '37 passenger car front end with a '40-'41 pickup cab and bed. It works!

This radical custom '39 coupe employs trends of the late '50s and early '60s, with canted '59 Chevy quad lights, lakes pipes frenched into the running boards, smoothed '49 Plymouth ripple bumpers and pinstriped flames.

Ford didn't make a roadster pickup after '32, but Rick Holgate built this one out of a '47 cab, '38 front clip and custom-built bed with '37 sides.

Here's an interesting combination that showed up at a swap meet in the '80s, though apparently built long ago. 1939 or '40 front clip has been mated to a roadster body from a '36 or '37, the last years for that body style, which is channeled over the frame. Wheel openings are trimmed for clearance.

Possibly the nicest thing that ever happened to a '40 Ford was connecting with Rudy Stoessel and Coachcraft, Ltd., in Hollywood. Rudy created this beautiful cabriolet in 1941. The handbuilt body placed the passenger compartment 12 inches to the rear of stock '40 position, with front fenders lengthened a like amount. The body is channeled over the frame, and the hood is sectioned to compensate. Running boards were omitted, a new grille center formed of round rod, '39 Lincoln front bumper and custom-built windshield are other features. Tex Myers rescued and restored this classic.

21

One of the wildest and most famous '40s ever built was The Matador by Bill Cushenberry. John Eichinger had this Matador replica in recent years. One-piece Studebaker windshield, a grille of tube sections mounted to a metal mesh, and scoops worked into the fender contours are a few of the changes.

The effect of channeling the '40 Deluxe body over the frame is a severe lowering without altering the ride, as chassis lowering does. Wheel housings must be opened up for wheel clearance. This neat coupe was built in the late '50s. Where is it now?

The very rounded curves of the '41-'48 Fords have attracted customizers for decades. Chopping the top is one popular modification. Larry Purcell kept the stock back window and angled the B-pillars forward. Bumpers were eliminated and '42-'48 taillights molded in down low. Headlights are frenched with '52-'54 Merc rims.

Don Hanlin modernized his '41 pickup in the '60s by tunneling four headlights into the rounded fenders. A lot of similar attempts didn't turn out this nicely.

The modern black-out treatment has been applied to this '41 convertible, the last Ford without quarter windows. Bumpers are removed, other trim painted body color with only spun aluminum wheel discs for contrast.

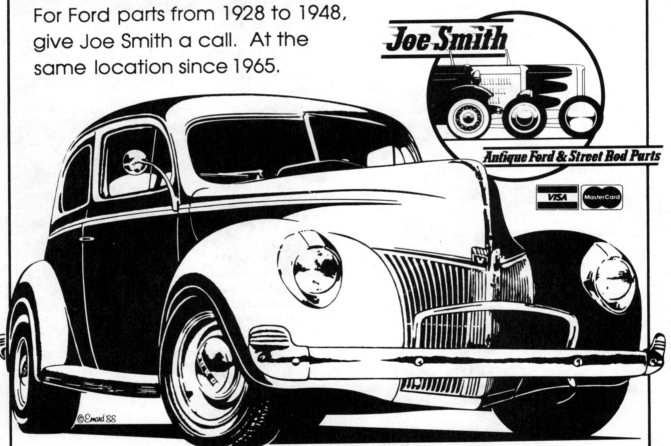

Louvers are used as a styling element on the rotund '41 sedan's deck lid. The job requires cutting skin from inner structure, punching louvers, then welding back together. 1959 Cadillac bullet taillights are tunneled low and rear pan rolled.

Unfinished '46-'48 showed up at a swap meet, and sports a '55-'56 Chevy pickup grille molded to the front, along with frenched headlights, shaved hood and filled pan.

Guy Root applied mild techniques to a '46-'48 convertible — shaved hood and deck, tunneled stock taillights, lakes pipes and Corvette hubcaps. There were lots of Fords similar to this in the '50s.

Modern look was applied to this '47 convertible by Gerry Charvat, with Z-28 wheels in radiused, flaired openings, Cordoba headlight rims and complete dechroming except for stock grille bars.

Paint schemes were wild in the '70s, and one of the wildest was this paneled job in several candy colors, designed and executed by Roger Peters on his '46 business coupe.

FAT FRAMES

by LeRoi Tex Smith

Fat Ford frames are strong, nearly bullet-proof. But they are not as strong as some other American car units of the same period. And for good reason. Through 1948, Ford continued to build a frame and suspension combination that was effective, but rather primitive. The hot rod fraternity long ago dubbed this the "buggy spring" arrangement.

Essentially, the frame is a platform that sits atop the springs on a centerline point of rotation. The front and rear transverse springs (buggy springs) mount to the frame on a centerline drawn through the frame front to rear. Additional attachments, such as the front and rear-end wishbones, are on the same centerline. Without shock absorber restraints, the frame/body will roll easily about this central mounting point. For this reason, the frame does not need to be as beefy as something using corner-point semi-elliptic springs.

Frame dimensions for 1935-'40 Ford car, and 1935-'41 Ford pickup truck.

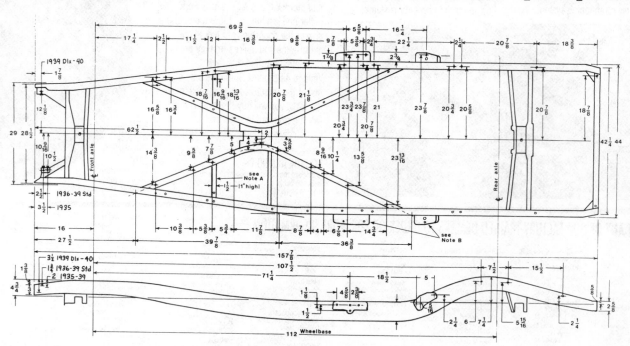

Note A: Used on convertible and station wagon only.
Note B: Not used on pickup trucks.

In 1932, Ford engineers started to design the frame so that the body could be deeper (bottom to top) as well as set closer to the ground. To do this, the frame became swaybacked. But there is a limit to how much drop can be built into a frame, and by 1935 this limit was pretty much determined. From then on, the emphasis was on gaining passenger room, which meant minor wheelbase changes and location of the engine forward over the front crossmember. Very little was changed in frame design and construction technique. However, there are enough differences so that it is not possible for a direct interchange of a 1937 frame with a 1947 frame. There are enough similarities, however, for interchange between close years, say a 1937 with a 1939, with modifications.

All of the frames from 1935 on are of double wall construction, with the X-member continuing inside the outer rails to the front and rear crossmembers. As a general rule, it is not necessary to box these frames (weld a steel plate to the open face C-section), but most builders usually add a box area at the rear crossmember, and from the firewall area forward to the front crossmember. The double wall frame is strong enough in stock form to handle all of the modern small block engines, but big block engines definitely call for frame boxing.

The major problem with these frames is age. The older the frame, the more likely the chance there will be rust. Especially between the double walls, and anywhere a body mounting box is riveted to the outside of the main rails. Quite often, there will be stress cracks where the front and rear crossmembers attach to the rails, and on the crossmembers around the central spring U-bolt points. This deterioration must be repaired before the frame can be used for a project.

Start any frame restoration by diagonal measuring of the frame and by checking for frame twist (as viewed from front and rear). Repair any alignment problems before continuing. When repairing a frame section by adding a repair piece or welding one portion of rail to the other, always avoid a straight across weld. Instead, make a V or zig-zag splice, and include a fishplate or box section to the inside of the frame. Weld up cracks. Do not grind all the weld from a frame repair, since that will remove most of the weld area strength. If cosmetics is vital, make the major weld on the inside of the frame. MIG welding on frames is not recommended for the amateur. In such a case, an arc welder is much better, or a TIG welder. After welding, check frame measurements again.

Working on the frame is one of the dirtiest jobs in building a car. Make it easier by sandblasting the frame before doing any welding, and keep the frame dry until the frame can be painted, to prevent future rusting. Use one of the new two-part etching primers on the frame, and a two-part catalyzed paint for maximum paint life.

It is possible to modify fat Ford frames with front clips and rear clips, or even to substitute an entirely different car frame for the Ford original. But this kind of frame modification is easier on 1941 and later Fords than on the 1935-'40 models. This is partly because of engine location, and partly because of the method of mounting the radiator and front sheetmetal clip. It doesn't mean the work can't be done on the earlier cars, only that it is easier on the later models.

Fat Ford frames are pretty straight forward stuff. They require patience more than engineering expertise, and this is an area where the amateur and professional alike will hate the drudgery involved. But, once finished with a frame, there is a tremendous feeling of accomplishment.

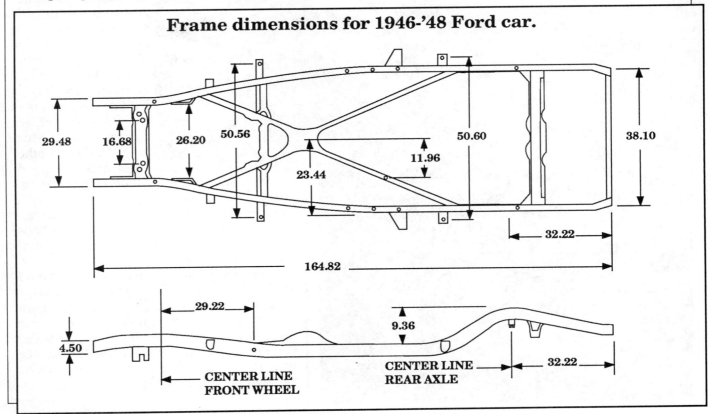

Frame dimensions for 1946-'48 Ford car.

WEEDETR'S REPRO CHASSIS

by Rich Johnson

Goodguys '40 convertible giveaway car was built on a WEEDETR '40 Ford reproduction frame. Rolling chassis is shown here, complete with dummy engine and transmission, and sporting a set of Boyds wheels.

What we have here is a fine example of a reproduction 1935-'40 Ford chassis, made by WEEDETR Street Rod Components, long-time maker of fat stuff, whose concern is for driveable street rods. According to company president Dale Caulfield, they engineer these chassis with an emphasis on good ride and handling characteristics, and to be sufficiently durable to handle day to day highway chores. At the same time, show quality is highly important. In fact, this particular chassis was used under the Goodguys '40 convertible giveaway car.

These '35-'40 Ford frames are exact reproductions of original frames, but with some changes made to accommodate a variety of engine/transmission swaps. Front and rear frame sections are boxed for added strength. An original type X-member is used for convenience of mounting the body and accessories, although the X-member is widened for increased transmission clearance. Access holes in the frame permit routing of exhaust pipes and plumbing.

The basic frame consists of the side rails, X-member, rear cross-member, and boxed front and rear sections. Also included are cowl braces for convertible and woodie models, along with braces between the X-member and main rails. Options include crossmembers to mount either dropped axle, Mustang II or some other aftermarket independent front suspension systems. There are also setups for installing Ford or Chevy engine and transmission mounts, parallel leaf or coilover/triangulated 4-link rear suspensions, exhaust systems, trailer hitches, brake pedal and master cylinder mounts.

Even though these frames are '35-'40 models, WEEDETR has many chassis components available for Fords of '35-'48 vintage. If you want to get in touch with WEEDETR, contact them at 1355 Vista Way, Red Bluff, CA 96080; (916) 527-2040. Now let's take a look at this neat piece that eventually found its home under the Goodguys '40 convertible.

Stripped down chassis gives us a good view of the boxed front and rear frame sections. Boxing adds strength in these critical areas where engine weight, torque movement, and suspension forces are concentrated.

Rear brake plumbing involves a Magoo plumbing kit. Note that there are holes in the frame to facilitate routing brake and fuel lines. Rear suspension was designed with inboard springs. Spring mounts are high on the frame rails, helping to achieve a lower ride height without the use of lowering blocks.

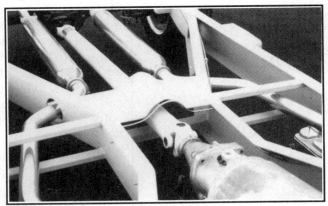

To accommodate a variety of engine/transmission swaps, the X-member has been opened up quite a bit. This type of X-member also serves as a containment cage for the forward end of the driveshaft in the event a U-joint lets go. Note the slick way the exhaust system is routed through the X-member rails.

Bracketry is available for installing a below-the-floorboard master cylinder and brake pedal setup. When the exhaust system is routed nearby, a heat shield is installed to protect the master cylinder. Brake system plumbing can be routed along the frame members for a clean installation.

A Rock Valley gas tank nestles between the rear frame rails, and a relocated gas filler neck was employed.

For this car, a Kugel Komponents front suspension was installed. WEEDETR engine mounts are in place, as are the radiator supports and front fender mounts. Note the hole in the right hand box plate — this is a pre-plumbed fuel port.

X-MEMBER SUPPORT

by Rich Johnson

Installation of a Pete & Jake's '35-'40 Ford X-member support restores the torsional strength of the stock cradle, and the unit can be installed either with or without the stock cradle still in place. If the stock cradle is still in the X-member, the new support unit is installed and then the original cradle is simply cut out with a torch.

One critical aspect of installation is that the frame must be level side-to-side at both the front and rear before the X-member support is welded or bolted in place. If not, the frame may have a twist (one corner lower than the others). It is also important to verify that the frame is of stock width and measures the same from opposite corners of the frame in an "X" pattern. These measurements will ensure that the frame is not only level, but also square.

The support slips in between the X-member channels from the rear, and the fit should be snug. Use a rubber hammer to drive the support as far forward as possible. If the stock cradle has already been removed, check the frame width at the body bolt holes indicated on the accompanying illustration. Also check the relationship of the top edge of the X-member channels to the top edge of the frame rails. The X-member should be 5/8" lower than the frame rails at the body bolt holes.

The support may be either welded or bolted into the X-member. To bolt the support in place, drill holes through both the X-member and the support at the same time, to assure alignment. Drill 8 holes, one at each end of the horizontal flanges of the support channels. Measure in approximately 5/8" from the ends of the channel and approximate center of the rail. Drill holes 3/8" diameter and use fine-thread bolts for the installation.

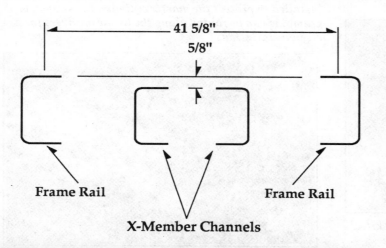

41 5/8"

5/8"

Frame Rail   **Frame Rail**

X-Member Channels

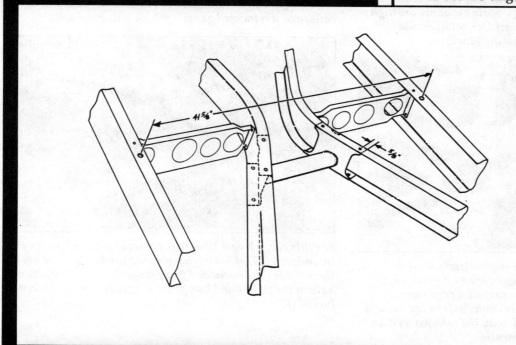

Your ... "Do-it-Yourself Parts Store"

Brake Pedal/ Master Cylinder Mount Assembly

The safety of a dual master cylinder with the ease of operation of power brakes. This WEEDETR brake pedal/ master cylinder mount assembly is designed to mount a Japanese built Bendix booster/ master cylinder. This unit will also mount a Ford non-power dual master cylinder. Fits '35-48 Ford frames as a bolt-in. Includes mounting hardware, brake light switch bracket and instructions.

#2050: 1935-40 Ford $126.00
#3050: 1941-48 Ford $126.00

WEEDETR ... Your Low Fat Headquarters And Parts That Fit!

'35-'40 Reproduction Frames

Stronger and Better than Henry's ...

The WEEDETR Street Rod Components reproduction '35-40 Ford frame is designed to make the construction of your project as easy as possible. These frames are exact reproductions of original frames but with the right changes in the right places. WEEDETR uses an original type X-member for the convenience of attaching the body and accessories. The basic frame consists of the side rails, X-member, rear crossmember and boxing front & rear. Also included are the cowl braces for convertible and woodie along with the braces between the X-member and the main rails.
From $1,850.00

Parallel Leaf Rear Suspension Kit

The WEEDETR exclusive designed parallel leaf rear suspension kit for '35-40 Fords mounts the springs inside the frame rails for the low ride height without the need for lowering blocks. Kit consists of weld-in or bolt-in forward spring mounts, bolt-in rear spring mounts, standard or reversed eye springs, U-bolts, pads to weld to rear end housing, spring plates, shackles, mounting hardware and instructions.
Complete ... **from $310.00**

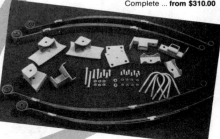

Exhaust System

This WEEDETR designed exhaust system fits all 1935 thru 1940 Ford chassis with small block Chevy engines using stock center dump "rams horn" exhaust manifolds. System fits inside frame for better chassis to ground clearance. Complete 2" mild steel system requires no welding or bending to install. Complete with all mounting hardware. Exhaust systems for '41-48 Fords also available.

#2170: '35-40 system $275.00
#3170: '41-48 system $275.00

Trailer Hitch

Class I hitches for '35-48 Fords. The '35-40 unit is a bolt-in that will fit frames with stock or after market fuel tanks. Receiver fits flush with the rear of the body. Specify year and body style for correct fit. The '41-48 unit is a bolt-in that is designed to fit using stock fuel tanks. Unit mounts using special supplied crossmember and stock rear spring crossmember. Hitches available in conjunction with our parallel leaf rear suspension. Draw bars available on special order.

From $145.00

Front Spring

New reversed eye springs for '35-41 Ford front suspensions. These springs are the only ones available today incorporating the **moly-slider slider buttons** with **tapered spring leafs** to produce the best ride quality available for early Ford front suspensions $135.00

Best Quality on the Market

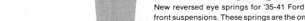

Sway Bar

Adjustable rear stabilizer bar. Arm lengths are adjustable to aid in fine tuning the handling characteristics of your chassis set-up. Kits available to fit '33-48 Ford and many others. $124.00

WEEDETR Street Rod Components
1355 Vista Way, Red Bluff, CA 96080 • 916/527-2040
Member • NSRA •SREA • SEMA •

GM CHASSIS UNDER A FAT FORD

by Steven W. Sutton

Much as I would like to accept the accolades for devising this frame/body swap of a late model GM chassis under a pre-'49 Ford, it was only possible with the help and information provided by Dean W. Bordner, of International Automotive, 2617 Meyer Rd., Ft. Wayne, Indiana 46803.

Based upon his information, I was able to modify the frame and, of course, make changes of my own, but I had the body on the frame in very little time.

The frame I used was a '72 Chevelle 4-door sedan. This frame has a wheelbase of 116", which was very close to the 115" wheelbase of the '47 Ford. I have been told that all intermediate size GM products (Chevelle, LeMans, Cutlass, Skylark, etc.) from 1966 through 1977 are basically the same. However, I suggest that very careful measurements be taken before purchasing the donor car. Differences may occur in wheelbase, tread width, steering mount location, etc.

The Chevelle used for this swap was complete with power disc brakes, power steering, automatic transmission, V8 engine, and air conditioning. I was able to use all of this except the air conditioning, because it was too bulky and heavy. I also used the Chevelle tilt steering column, power brake booster and master cylinder, and the brake pedal mounting bracket between the firewall and dashboard.

The following instructions are designed to be as complete and simple as possible. There may be variations to each individual application, so make sure that you decide how the final project is to appear before executing any final work. To obtain the best results, it is vital to double and triple check measurements and fit.

1. Assuming that you have a complete late model GM car, remove the body and sheetmetal, gas tank, etc. from the frame. Degrease as needed, leaving the engine, transmission and driveline in the frame.

2. Determine the wheelbase you need, and shorten or lengthen the frame as needed.

3. You will need 20 feet of 3"x4" thick-wall box tubing, 6 feet of 1-1/2"x2" angle iron, and 4 feet of 3"x3" light-wall box tubing.

4. Block all four tires so that the frame does not roll. Block up the transmission, and remove the transmission crossmember. Save the crossmember for later.

5. Notch the frame at all four corners (as indicated in the drawing), leaving only the bottom of the corners intact. Then cut the 3"x4" box tubing to the desired length and lay in place.

6. Weld the ends and insides of the new rails at each corner. Make provisions to assure that the frame doesn't warp while welding.

7. Trim the old frame sections away, as shown in the drawing. Heat and bend the overlap on the outside of the new rails (about 8 inches should be enough), and weld into place.

8. Cut the old transmission crossmember to fit between the new rails, and mark location on the rails. Cut the 1-1/2"x2" angle iron to form mounting brackets, and weld these to the rails where marked. Cut two more pieces of angle iron and weld these to the old crossmember. At this point, you should be able to drill two holes in each bracket and mount the completed assembly.

9. Trial fit the body, centering the rear wheelwell over the rear axle. Determine where rear floor sheetmetal needs to be trimmed, and remove only the amount necessary.

10. Locate the body mounts at the rear of the trunk floor, and shorten the rear frame horns to allow installation of the new 3"x3" tube crossmember and angle iron for the body mount. This could also serve as rear gas tank mount.

11. Now you will be able to almost lower the body completely over the frame. Front frame horns are still going to interfere. You will need to determine what you are going to use for a front bumper, if anything. If you plan to use the stock bumper and pan, you will need to make a bracket that will mount to the front of the short-

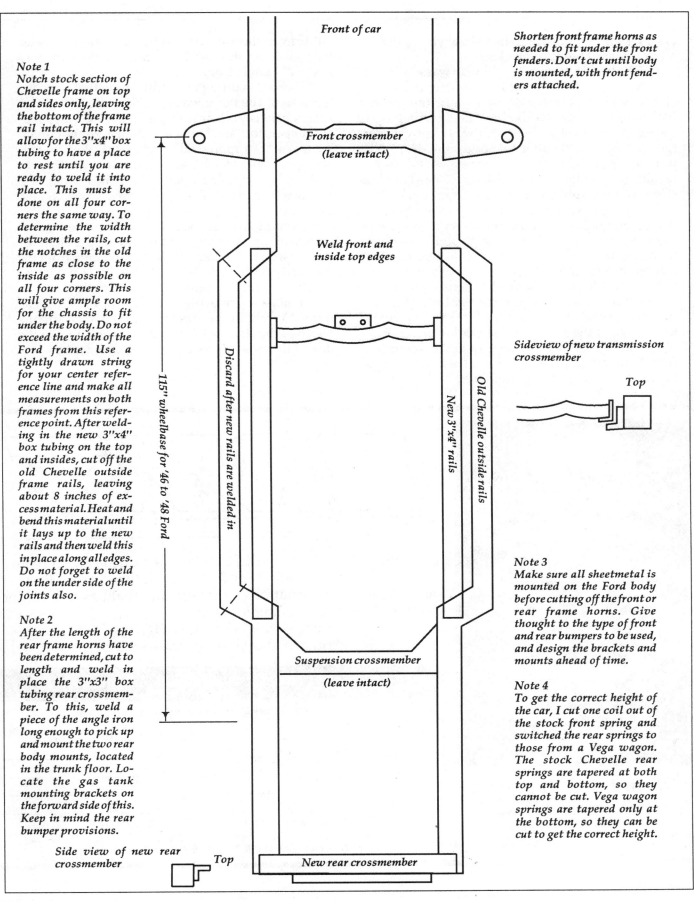

Note 1
Notch stock section of Chevelle frame on top and sides only, leaving the bottom of the frame rail intact. This will allow for the 3"x4" box tubing to have a place to rest until you are ready to weld it into place. This must be done on all four corners the same way. To determine the width between the rails, cut the notches in the old frame as close to the inside as possible on all four corners. This will give ample room for the chassis to fit under the body. Do not exceed the width of the Ford frame. Use a tightly drawn string for your center reference line and make all measurements on both frames from this reference point. After welding in the new 3"x4" box tubing on the top and insides, cut off the old Chevelle outside frame rails, leaving about 8 inches of excess material. Heat and bend this material until it lays up to the new rails and then weld this in place along all edges. Do not forget to weld on the under side of the joints also.

Note 2
After the length of the rear frame horns have been determined, cut to length and weld in place the 3"x3" box tubing rear crossmember. To this, weld a piece of the angle iron long enough to pick up and mount the two rear body mounts, located in the trunk floor. Locate the gas tank mounting brackets on the forward side of this. Keep in mind the rear bumper provisions.

Side view of new rear crossmember

Top

Front of car

Front crossmember
(leave intact)

Weld front and inside top edges

Discard after new rails are welded in

New 3"x4" rails

Old Chevelle outside rails

115" wheelbase for '46 to '48 Ford

Suspension crossmember
(leave intact)

New rear crossmember

Shorten front frame horns as needed to fit under the front fenders. Don't cut until body is mounted, with front fenders attached.

Sideview of new transmission crossmember

Top

Note 3
Make sure all sheetmetal is mounted on the Ford body before cutting off the front or rear frame horns. Give thought to the type of front and rear bumpers to be used, and design the brackets and mounts ahead of time.

Note 4
To get the correct height of the car, I cut one coil out of the stock front spring and switched the rear springs to those from a Vega wagon. The stock Chevelle rear springs are tapered at both top and bottom, so they cannot be cut. Vega wagon springs are tapered only at the bottom, so they can be cut to get the correct height.

ened GM frame rails, and also allow you to use the stock (old car) bumper brackets.

12. The body mount at the firewall was made from a piece of the 3"x4" tubing that was cut open to sit about two inches above the new frame rail and one inch to the outside. The body mount just in from of the rear wheelwell was one that was removed from the Ford frame and bolted to the new rail. The mount just forward of that was made of the 3"x4" tubing and welded perpendicular to the side rail. Then I used the stock '47 Ford rubber biscuits to mount the body.

That pretty much covers most of the modification necessary to allow the frame to fit completely under the sheetmetal of a '47 Ford coupe body. Following are some areas of concern and things that I learned during the construction.

1. I was able to use the stock '47 gas tank, but had to move it forward about 6 inches. I made a front mounting bracket from strap steel that was welded to the tops of the spring and shock towers.

2. You will need to make a radiator mount and front fender mounting cage, since the original radiator used a cage assembly to mount both it and the entire front sheetmetal to the frame. I used a '65 Mustang radiator, mounted to a cage made from 1-1/2"x1-1/2" angle iron.

3. The only cutting or modification that I needed to make to the body was to relieve the front inner splash panels to clear the Chevelle front independent suspension, and to the rear floor area just behind the rear seat supports. This was to clear the Chevelle rear spring and shock towers, and was cut away the width of the floor and about 18 inches wide. This area was then replaced with a sheetmetal box, welded into place.

4. I was able to use the stock '72 Chevelle exhaust system all the way back to the rear suspension.

5. I used stock Chevelle shifting linkage from the column, and tried to use all stock parts wherever possible, as this makes things much easier.

6. Before making the four cuts in the Chevelle frame to weld in the 3"x4" box tubing, measure the width of the stock '47 Ford frame to ensure that the new rails are as close to that measurement as possible.

LATE CHASSIS SWAP

by Gerry Charvat

Chassis swaps are becoming popular with hot rodders. People have discovered that the wrecking yards are full of perfectly good late model chassis that can be modified to fit under early bodies. The greatest benefit of the swap is that suddenly you have an early car with modern ride and handling characteristics.

A good example of a chassis swap for fat Fords is the one we illustrate here. This involves transplanting a late '60s to early '70s GM mid-size 115-inch wheelbase chassis under the classic body of a fat Ford. The really neat thing about this swap is that anyone with welding ability can do it, and end up with a very inexpensive modern chassis. Very safe, with super handling. And you have the neat options of GM power steering, great brakes, modern electrical system, etc.

This is different from the type of frame/chassis swap Dick Dean does on the west coast for '49 and later Mercs, in that he has to make practically no frame modifications. Here, we have to work up a new central frame section. But it isn't very difficult. All you need to remember is to make all of the welds very good, and use strong gussets. Measure and re-measure as you proceed, and you won't get into trouble.

I have a rod/custom shop, and if you want a set of drawings and instructions, with a material list, I sell that for $50. More information can be obtained from: Hot Rod Shop, 5706 Industrial Road, Fort Wayne, Indiana 46825; (219)482-7473.

We're talking super zoomie and double-throw-down trick here, folks. This is the GM 4-door mid-size 115-inch wheelbase frame (late '60s, early '70s) with side rails modified for the fat Ford crowd. Stock Chevelle exhaust system bolts in. Front frame horns must be modified for chosen radiator support.

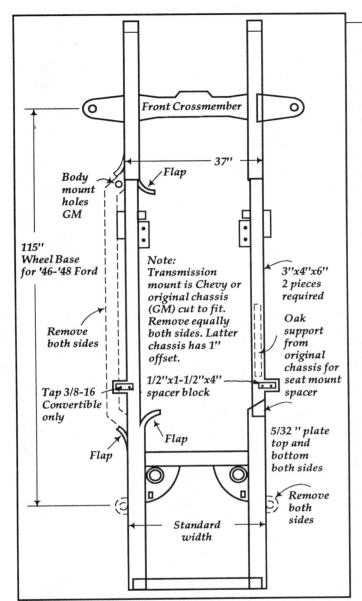

Front Crossmember

37"

Body mount holes GM

Flap

115" Wheel Base for '46-'48 Ford

Remove both sides

Note: Transmission mount is Chevy or original chassis (GM) cut to fit. Remove equally both sides. Latter chassis has 1" offset.

3"x4"x6" 2 pieces required

Oak support from original chassis for seat mount spacer

1/2"x1-1/2"x4" spacer block

Tap 3/8-16 Convertible only

Flap

Flap

5/32" plate top and bottom both sides

Remove both sides

Standard width

Once the GM chassis is stripped, locate two pieces of 3x4-inch, 1/8-inch tubing that measure 6 feet 2 inches long (each). These will be used to straighten the perimeter frame.

This hole is 11-1/2 inches behind the front crossmember and is a measurement starting point. Actual cut will be 5 to 6 inches behind this, giving an overlapping flap.

The author and wife Sandy do some garage dreaming with Ford convert body that will fit on the 1968-'72 GM chassis, giving super ride, late brakes, etc.

New frame insert is laid on top of the stock frame and lines drawn to serve as a cutting guide.

Open the inside and top flaps like this. New frame insert will slide inside the original frame. At this point, open up the original frame at rear area in the same way so the new frame rail insert can be jockeyed into position. Before going further, be sure the chassis is suspended at 6 points (at least) and level. Make cross and diagonal measurements of stock chassis for later reference.

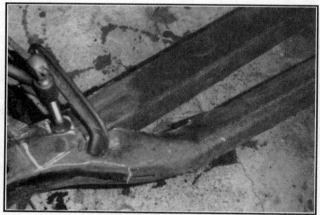

Insert new tube in frame at rear. Position in front so that the tube is inside the opening. C-clamp the tube in place and form the overlapping flaps to fit inside and top of tube. Note: Trim upper inside rear corner of new tube so it will clear indentation in the stock chassis. This cut is about 2 inches long.

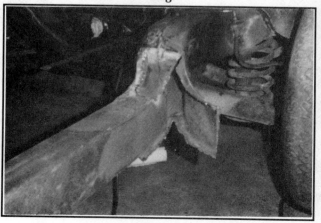

Lower front ends of new frame tubes are cut to fit inside sloping stock frame. Cut starts about 4-1/2 inches back, tapering to a 2-1/4 inch width.

With front and rear of tube inserted in stock chassis, the flaps can be welded. Check reference measurements often. The kickout portion of the original frame perimeter will be cut off and discarded.

Make sure that the chassis welds are excellent. Your safety depends upon them.

Left-Perimeter rail is cut so that there is overlap material to weld to the new tube, front and rear.

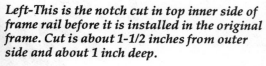

Left-This is the notch cut in top inner side of frame rail before it is installed in the original frame. Cut is about 1-1/2 inches from outer side and about 1 inch deep.

Below-Inserted inside the stock frame at the rear, the new tubing has overlaps from the original frame. These are heated and worked to fit the new tubing, and held in place with big C-clamps.

Left-After measurements show everything is still straight and square, the new tube is welded in place at the rear.

Above-Overlap flaps on inside and outside of the rail insert piece ensure maximum strength for the area. Additional plate can be made for the top of the rail junctions front and back, if desired. Such plates are definitely advised on the bottom at both points.

Left-Rear frame extensions must be shortened for the 1941-'48 Fords. This final distance will be 32-1/2 inches from the centerline of the rear axle to the rear of the frame extension. On some chassis, there will be a 3-inch upward curve at the rear of this extension.

Right-A 1977-'79 Monza gas tank works well and comes with an electric fuel pump. Front mount for the tank straps can be made from 1-inch square tubing. Filler neck is routed to fit the Ford fender.

Below-Remember those 3-inch extensions on some stock chassis. This is exactly how high the Ford body is over the frame extension. If needed, mounts can be made of steel stock that is bent to shape.

Right-New cowl mounting pads are built up to fit the particular body being used.

Above-A couple of body mounting brackets are needed at the rear. This will vary according to the body being used.

Right-Here the chassis has been painted, but front of frame horns have not been modified. Don't cut them until you have decided on what radiator support system you will use.

Transmission mount is cut off on each end to just fit inside frame rails. This mount sits on 2x2-inch, 1/8-inch angle iron supports welded to frame rails. Bolt the trans mount in place for easier transmission service later.

The radiator core support will be different from the Ford style. Fender splash aprons must be trimmed away for clearance, but this allows use of a larger late model radiator.

If you want to use the 1965-'67 GM radiator core support, cut the front frame horns as shown and make a mounting bracket.

Now you have a chassis that is ready for the body. Modern all the way around, and at a very reasonable cost.

Upper left-Ford convertibles have a special cowl area brace off the frame. This can be duplicated and added to the modified frame rails.

Above-Special splash aprons for inside of rear fenders should be used. Make some up if you don't have them already. Relocate the gas filler neck as needed.

Left-Power brake assembly mounts to the firewall with plenty of room. Steering mounts at firewall slightly higher than original, in order to align properly with the stock GM gearbox. GM automatic transmission linkage can also be used.

**CONTE ENTERPRISES • 28002 110 AVE. E., DEPT. MX., GRAHAM, WA 98338
(206) 847-4666**

INDEPENDENCE FOR ALL

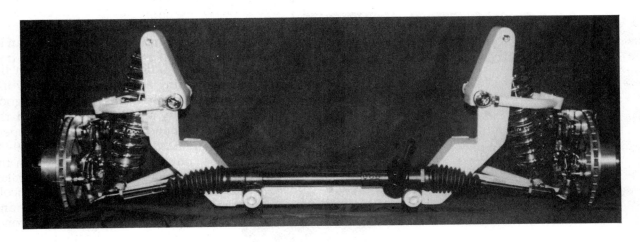

This is one of several new front suspension kits for the heavier street rods and pro-street rides. This new design uses a longer 4-inch stroke coil over shock that lets the suspension work properly, giving you a much better ride, excellent handling, and greatly reduces bump steer. The crossmember and A-arms are hand-built, we use GM spindles, rotors and calipers (or JFZ calipers) and pinto rack and pinion. The 28-31 Ford uses a rear-mounted rack and sway bar. Complete front suspension weight is approximately 180lbs. with rotors and calipers.

The suspension unit pictured was designed for the 35-40 Ford's. Below is a list of what we have designed suspension kits for. If your car is not included it may be in the planning stages or one of the crossmembers we have may be very close to fitting your car if your frame rails are 24"-35" wide outside. If you have any questions about your application please call. We also guarantee final spring rate on the finished car. Thank you for your interest in my product.

READY FIT APPLICATIONS ARE:

**ALDAN
SHOCKS**

37-39 Chevy car
40-48 Chevy car (bolt in)
55-57 Chevy (sub frame)
28-31 Ford
35-40 Ford

40-54 Chevy Pick-up
55-59 Chevy Pick-up
48-52 Ford F-1
53-56 Ford F-100
57-66 Ford F-100

**JFZ
BRAKES**

FOR FULL INFORMATION, PLEASE SEND $2.00 TO HELP COVER COST.

43

FRONT SUSPENSION

by LeRoi Tex Smith

Mustang II front suspension swaps are popular for fat Fords. It's an excellent way to improve ride and handling as well as picking up modern steering and brake components. This Mustang II unit was installed under David Winter's pro street '40 (covered in greater detail later in this book), but similar swaps can be made under any fat Ford.

The Ford buggy spring suspension used through the 1948 model year cars was basic, strong, and is usable under any rod or custom. It can be highly modified, or it can be replaced by some other system. But the 1948 units are not exactly carbon copies of the 1935 units. There are slight differences, although there is a large degree of interchangeability through the years.

The original transverse leaf front suspension, introduced in 1935, has the spring mounted ahead of the axle. In succeeding years, the basic design remained almost unchanged. The spring length changed slightly, and measurements/configuration of the wishbone changed. In 1939, hydraulic brakes were first introduced to the front end.

The stock type Ford front suspension can be an excellent unit. If the springs are cleaned of rust, and Teflon inserted between the leafs, spring action is dramatically improved. Couple this with some good heavy duty shock absorbers, and the ride and handling of this front suspension are hard to improve. The 1939-'48 front spindles will interchange on the older axles, allowing hydraulic brakes rather than mechanicals. The Lincoln brakes (Bendix) also interchange, and are better still. Late model Ford Econoline drum brakes can be modified to fit the '35-'48 axles. Even the Buick finned drums of the late Fifties and early Sixties can be bolted to the Ford hubs and backing plates, with modifications for improved braking.

Most builders of fat Fords who opt to keep the original type front suspension also want to lower the car. There are two very quick ways to do this. The front crossmember can be flattened to effectively lower the relationship between the axle and the frame, but take care not to get an interference between the tie rods and the frame. The stock beam axle can be replaced by a dropped axle. Again, watch for tie rod interference. The crossmember drop will account for upwards of 2 inches of lowering. Axles can go as much as 4 inches, although a 2-1/2 or 3-inch dropped axle is probably the all around choice.

Caution: When dropping the front end either way, the relationship of the cross-steering tie rod to the main tie rod will change. In the stock original position, the main tie rod will pass through the pitman arm steering tie rod mounting point when the front axle goes up and down under normal conditions. Because of this, there is no bump steer (the steering suddenly jerks to one side as the suspension travels up or down). When the relative position of the spindle arms change, the cross-steering must also be modified to preclude bump steer.

If there is at least 4 inches of travel between the axle and the frame, the ride will be comfortable. Even so, the car will bottom out on severe bumps. Less clearance than this, and the car can be uncomfortable and unpleasant to drive.

The popular 4-bar drag link (wishbone replacement) combination, available from street rod suppliers, works very well on fat Fords.

In recent years, it has become popular to replace the Ford transverse spring front suspension with some kind of independent front suspension, usually a derivative of the Mustang/Pinto. While it is possible to carefully trim the Mustang sheetmetal and mount this to the Ford frame, it is usually much better to either make up a new Mustang A-arm crossmember or buy

a kit. Other types of IFS have been used, such as the bolt-on Pacer front end, but the Mustang/Pinto assembly seems to be the favorite. In addition, several rod shop suppliers make up their own independent suspension components.

The difference between a Ford type front end (properly set up) and an independent system is mostly in ride and handling on certain concrete highways. In some cases, the expansion joints of these cement highways seem to be in phase with the shorter wheelbase early fat Fords, causing a kind of pitching motion in the car. With loose, soft springing and firm shocks, this is not really a problem. The IFS front end tends to nullify this pitching motion. In some cases (but not all), an IFS also tends to improve cornering, allowing the car to drive harder and deeper into a curve. This is a property of the improved unsprung weight in an IFS, center of gravity shift, etc. Generally speaking, it is good to get a ride in cars with both types of suspension before making a decision.

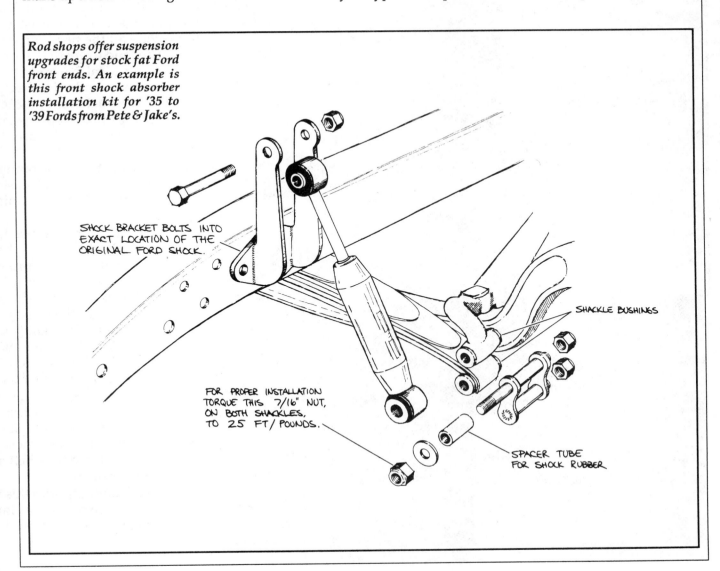

Rod shops offer suspension upgrades for stock fat Ford front ends. An example is this front shock absorber installation kit for '35 to '39 Fords from Pete & Jake's.

SHOCK BRACKET BOLTS INTO EXACT LOCATION OF THE ORIGINAL FORD SHOCK.

SHACKLE BUSHINGS

FOR PROPER INSTALLATION TORQUE THIS 7/16" NUT, ON BOTH SHACKLES, TO 25 FT/POUNDS.

SPACER TUBE FOR SHOCK RUBBER

BUTCH'S 4-BAR FRONT

Fat Ford builders of 1935 through '40 persuasion have the option of installing a 4-bar front suspension system from Butch's Rod Shop. Because of changes to frame design, the 4-bar system doesn't work well with '41 to '48 Fords, due to the fact that the links would interfere with the tires during full-lock turns. Oh well, too bad, but at least the earlier guys can have fun with this stuff.

Butch's Rod Shop has been in the fat Ford chassis business since 1975, and usually has all the goodies a do-it-yourselfer on a budget needs. Everything from complete chassis to bits and pieces can be ordered from Butch, who claims to have developed the very first workable 4-link front suspension system for the '35-'40 Fords, which is what we're taking a look at here. This kit was developed in 1978, and has been their most popular fat Ford front suspension system.

This photo shows Butch's complete '40 Ford chassis, filled with all sorts of hardware. But focussing attention on the front end, notice the state of the art 4-link system. It's a package that has been engineered to provide all the necessary component clearances and to get the car down in the front for an ideal hot rod stance. Included in the kit is a standard 4" dropped front axle (1/4" wall thickness and 2" outside diameter tubing), that drops the car 3" to 3-1/2". An additional 1-1/2" of drop can be ordered for those who don't mind clipping their lawn with the front bumper, and that kit includes a pair of custom dropped steering arms that are required for tie rod clearance.

The kit comes with seamless bars that have stainless steel adjusters and urethane bushings. If the stock transverse spring is to be used, it must be shortened for installation, or a Posie Superslide reverse eye spring can be ordered as part of the package.

Also visible in the photo is the Pete and Jake's bolt-on '35 to '40 front shock kit. One note about this kit is that it will not fit with the stock '40 front sway bar. However, the photo clearly shows that a front sway bar has been neatly installed on this chassis. The trick was accomplished by installing Butch's new front stabilizer bar kit, specially designed to clear most all front tube shocks. Installation requires heli-arc welding of brackets to the axle tube.

Butch says the ride and handling with this kit is unexcelled. So, if you're looking for a time-tested 4-bar kit for a '35 to '40 Ford, you've just found it.

47

DROPPED SPINDLES

A very unusual method of dropping a stock Ford spindle is possible with a minimum of machine work and adaptation of some readily available AMC Pacer front bolt-on spindles.

Part of this job entails some welding on the Ford spindle. All 1935-'48 Ford spindles can be modified in this manner, although this is best left to a certified welder. A follow-up Magnaflux of the weld areas is a good idea for safety. But, extra safety comes by the lower Pacer spindle bolts passing through the stock Ford spindle face. Be sure to use the finest and strongest grade 8 bolts available (make sure you are not getting some imported Asian rip-off bolts.) Follow along to see how this is done.

Start by making a new plate to accept the Pacer spindle. This plate will use the top two Ford backing plate holes (in stock Ford spindle face). The plate is curved at the bottom edge to register on large diameter backing plate step on face of spindle. It is welded on this curve, and up either side, then across the back side. The Ford spindle bolt is cut off, and the entire face is ground flat.

The Pacer drum brakes shown are quite good for most street use. It is wise to include four bolts to hold each spindle in place. Some inner bolt head grinding may be needed for clearance of the hub. The vertical centerline of the wheel/tire combination is moved outward slightly with this swap.

This particular swap will drop the front end a bit over 2 inches. Might as well take the Ford spindles off and install new kingpins and bushings at the same time.
Below-The Pacer spindle is a bolt-on item, which is why it works so well with this swap. It offers both disc and drum brake options, as well.

Be sure to check for shock absorber clearance with wheels in full lock position each way. Total cost for a swap like this is very minor, and it is much easier than installing a dropped axle.

49

SPINDLE SWAP

by Tony Mills

Start the conversion by using the Econoline bushings pressed into the beam axle. A sleeve could be made, but the bushing works very well and seems to give a better fit than with sleeves.

Econoline spindles from 1961 through 1967 will work on pre-1949 Ford beam axles, or similar aftermarket units. The Econoline front end design was changed in 1968, so those and later years are not usable for our purposes.

Scrounge a set of spindles with good brakes and drums, or plan on modifying the spindles to accommodate discs. Also buy a new Econoline kingpin set.

Start by removing the old spindle bushings. Don't destroy them. A deep socket works great as a mandrel. Cut down the outside diameter of these bushings until they can be driven into the axle kingpin hole. I file them to fit, which should be snug. If you drive the bushing into the axle, don't pound directly on the bushing, as this will flair it out. Install one bushing from each end of the axle kingpin hole.

The axle is too wide to accept the Econoline spindles, so cut the axle boss with a disc grinder or machine tool. Usually about 1/16" will do. Install new bushings in the Econoline spindles and ream them to fit.

With a round file, clear the retaining bolt hole in the axle (kingpin retainer), as the bushings will protrude into the hole slightly. Take care, because the bushings are getting pretty thin by now. Use early Ford retaining bolt.

The spindles can now be installed on the axle. The steering arm needs a minor modification in order to accept the draglink. The hole is tapered from the bottom, causing the draglink and arm to interfere. Retaper this hole from the top and the draglink now clears. I use a "Bluepoint" number R121 reamer and make a cut halfway through the hole. This gives enough purchase for the tie rod. Any more and the tie rod end won't seat properly.

I ran into tie rod clearance problems with one combination of axle and radius rod. With a 2-1/2-inch dropped axle, the tie rod will not clear the stock wishbone. I solved this by notching and boxing the top of the wishbone and then reinforcing this with a gusset over the top. The tie rod passes through the hole thus provided, and no strength is lost in the wishbone.

Clearance is no problem with 4-inch dropped

axles, and hairpin or 4-bar radius rod setups don't have problems because of their design.

If you want disc brakes, the early Mustang type will fit. Some machine work will be needed on the spindle, but it is minor. The bearings are the same, so all that is required is to turn the spindle bolt back where the outer bearing rides. This will allow the Mustang hub bearings to work. Cut a few new threads on the shortened shaft. Fabricate a mounting bracket for the caliper, and you're set.

So, what do you gain with such a swap? How about late model brakes, wheel bolt pattern to match an 8- or 9-inch Ford rearend, parts available anywhere, no adapters or special parts required, no alignment problems, and you can do it all yourself (nearly). Finally, the cost is right. I've even gotten Econoline spindles free.

Two Econoline left-side spindles. The lower spindle is stock, while the upper spindle has the shortened spindle bolt for use with Mustang disc brake hubs and rotors. The difference is in outer/inner bearing centerlines. Most any machine shop can shorten the spindle bolt.

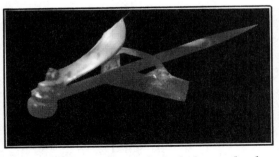

This vehicle used the 2-1/2-inch dropped axle, so a notch was cut in the wishbone for tie rod clearance, then a piece of plate stock was looped over the top for support.

The 1966-'67 type Econoline drum is finned. Note the draglink mounts on top of the steering arm.

The Mustang rotor and caliper is mounted to the Econoline spindle, which is, in turn, mounted to the beam axle. You'll have to make up your own caliper brackets, at least until an enterprising supplier starts making them.

If you've ever wondered about which spindles were used on different model years of fat Fords, these diagrams should be helpful.

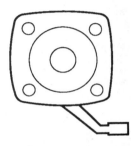

1937 -'41 Ford
Boss length: 2.375"
Pin size: 0.813"

1942 - '48
Boss Length: 2.375"
Pin size: 0.813"

TORSION BARS FOR FAT CARS

by Skip Readio

Mid-sized MoPars, from 1972 and later, have front suspensions that can be totally removed from the vehicle and still retain their geometry. They make a great swap for fat Fords . . . .

Mid-sized MoPars, from 1972 and later, have front suspensions that can be totally removed from the vehicle and still retain their geometry. They make a great swap for fat Fords, and are not too difficult to work with.

Unlike the earlier models that used the inner fender panel/frame section as a support for the upper control arm bushings, these units have a bracket bolted to the crossmember inside of the shock absorber that extends upward and inward, and is used to mount the upper control arm shaft.

The entire front crossmember is attached to the frame via an arrangement of four long bolts and four pairs of rubber insulators. When these are removed, the crossmember along with the steering box and all the steering linkage comes out. The rear anchors for the torsion bars are held up to the floor pan/frame by similar but smaller insulators and bolts.

To get one of these front ends out, loosen the torsion bar adjuster bolts up inside the lower control arms until the anchor bolts no longer contact the "finger" of the torsion bar front anchor. Go to the rear anchors and remove the retainer ring in the rear. Slide the torsion bars out and remove the rear anchor assembly while you're under there.

Up front, remove the upper control arm on one side and remove the support bracket for that control arm. If you don't take one side off, you won't be able to drop the suspension out as it wraps around the frame.

Disconnect the brake lines and the steering shaft. Remove the motor mount bolts and block the motor up under the oil pan. Remove the power steering pump from the front of the motor.

Put a jack or a couple of friends under the crossmember and remove the bolts holding it to the frame. That's all there is to it. Throw the crossmember, the torsion bars, and the rear anchors in the pickup and head for the quarter car wash.

Incidentally, you may want to grab the proportioning valve and master cylinder/brake booster while you're there. It would be nice to match the booster to the brakes you're getting.

Once the front end is cleaned up a bit, slide it under your rod and see what it looks like. Too wide? Well, narrowing it is a snap. There's enough flat surface to take at least six inches out of one of these front suspensions. When I cut mine, I scribed a line across the front and back in a horizontal plane, and I put a couple of lines across the top and bottom as well. Then I scribed Z-shaped cuts on each side. Matching the two halves to a straight cut seemed like a weaker joint, so I opted for the more difficult, but stronger, irregular joint.

One thing to keep in mind is that you want the mounting holes to end up on the outside of the frame. If they're too close together, the bolt will wind up going straight up the vertical part of the frame. This will require a bit of engineering to accommodate the threads, so be careful. Keep the front mounting holes just outside of the frame so you can affix something to run the bolt up into. In my case, the front end is under a fat Ford, 1940-'48 variety. Here, the MoPar crossmember can be narrowed 5 to 6 inches.

Once the cut was made, I aligned the scribe marks. They were straight, but weren't quite at right angles to the crossmember geometry. On the front side, one of them was inclined upward and the one on top angled back a bit. All I had to do was keep the lines parallel to each other to ensure a square fit.

Cut the center link the same amount as you cut the crossmember. If you're not certain how much you actually narrowed it (the fire wrench took a wide swath, or a little in-process alignment caused a little width to be added), measure the center-to-center distance between the steering box pitman shaft and the idler arm pivot. The outboard end of the pitman arm and the idler arm should be the same length. Cut the center link accordingly. The center link in these cars is massive and quite short. A qualified welder can shorten this easily and you shouldn't have to worry about it bending or breaking the way you would with a welded, dropped tie rod of days gone by.

The rear anchor is narrowed the same as the front and is bolted up to ears attached to the frame. The torsion bars have quite a bit of slop when it comes to locating the rear anchor, so find the midpoint and try to keep the anchor at it. To do this, just slide the narrowed anchor over the two torsion bars and see how far up or down it will actually move. This will give you room to adjust the crossmember later. Make sure that you keep the rear anchor centered side-to-side with respect to the front end. Again, not too difficult if you put a square up against the hex torsion bar socket's flange and make sure that the torsion bar is at right angles to the socket/anchor assembly.

I put this in my '40 frame and had to dimple the top of the frame a bit to clear the inner control arm bushing bosses. The front mounting bosses are separated from the '40 frame by the rubber insulator. The rears are way below the frame and slightly wider than the fronts. You'll have to fabricate an ear off the lower edge of the frame in the vicinity of the firewall, to extend the mounting surface down a few inches to meet the crossmember.

I had to remove the stock '40 front crossmember and install one up forward, for two reasons. One had to do with the addition of the new crossmember, and the other one was the oil pan on my new motor. Had I not had the oil pan clearance problem, I could have just notched the crossmember to clear the power steering box. The notch is significant, however, and will require that extra stiffening be added to the crossmember to compensate for the loss of metal around the new steering box.

When it comes to aligning the crossmember, go to the library and pick out the service manual for the year of manufacture of the car you got the crossmember from. In the FRAME section, will be all the collision repair specifications for leveling the frame. Usually, the front mounts are bolted in and the rear mounts shimmed to obtain the correct stance.

If you drastically alter the rear body stance at some later time, all you have to do is remove or add shims to the rear of the crossmember mounts.

If you don't plan on making any significant changes to the frame attitude, you can weld the crossmember right into the frame and eliminate the need for any stock crossmember strengthening or relocation. This approach also eliminates the need for keeping the crossmember bolts outside the frame, because you won't need them if you weld the crossmember to the frame.

One note regarding overall steering geometry. When the vehicle came from Detroit, the steering geometry was designed for a rather long wheelbase, compared to most older cars. If you draw an imaginary line, connecting the pivotal centerline of the spindle with the pivotal line of the outer tie rod end, that line should continue straight to the center of the rearend, when the tires are pointed straight ahead. When you narrow a front end, the intersection of these two lines moves forward.

If your wheelbase is shorter than the car you got the front end out of, you're in luck. It may end up that your rearend is close to or exactly where it belongs. If it is within an inch or so, I wouldn't worry about it. Your vehicle will handle much better in the rain or snow than one with the steering linkage out in front of the axle.

If you want to do some trigonometry, you can compare the track widths and wheelbases of both the late model and the street rod applications and come up with an optimum narrowing width before hand. (We're starting to get high-tech now). Looking at your suspension as two triangles (one for the left side and one for the right), the short leg is from the center of the crossmember out to the pivotal point of the spindle. At right angles to that line is the centerline of the vehicle, which is common to both triangles. The hypotenuse is the line connecting the pivotal point of the spindle with the center of the rear axle.

When you shorten the short leg (narrow the front crossmember), you shorten the hypotenuse and the long leg accordingly. Not very good at trig? Draw it out to scale on graph paper. It works just as well.

GIBBON T-BAR KIT

courtesy of George Packard

Skip Readio has told us how to pirate the torsion bar front end from MoPar products for use on early Fords. Now we'll take a look at a trick kit that has been put together by Gibbon Fiberglass. This is a kit that sells for $350 and will accept front suspension components from 1975-'78 Dodge Charger, Coronet, Superbee, or 1973-'74 Plymouth Belvedere, GTX, Road Runner, or Satellite. The rack and pinion steering will fit from 1981-'83 Dodge Aries, same years of Plymouth Reliant, or '83 Dodge passenger cars. Cross steering can be from any GM Saginaw medium or full size car of the 1970s, manual or power.

All of this will fit Fords, 1935 through 1940, and probably later Fords as well as other fat fender cars, but we haven't had a chance to check them out yet.

The big advantage of the kit is that minimum frame cutting is required, and the new crossmember is very narrow. You end up with a good wheel track width. Another major advantage is that the front ride height is adjustable, by cranking the torsion bars up or down.

When installing, leave the original crossmember in place. While this kit is designed to be a bolt-in, there will be a bit of grinding from one frame to the next. The kit comes with full instructions, showing what original frame holes to use, etc. Once the crossmember is located by these frame holes, it is welded in place. You'll have to make a couple of cuts on the original crossmember rear lip for lower control arm clearance.

The rear crossmember is for location of the torsion bar aft ends, and the idea is to get the bars in the same relative location as they were on the Chrysler product. This crossmember is also welded in place.

That's it! Bolt on the MoPar A-arms, install the torsion bars, and you're in business, with disc brakes as a plus and either 4-1/2 or 5-inch wheel bolt pattern.

You can use Saginaw manual or power steering, or MoPar rack and pinion steering, manual or power.

For full information, call Gibbon Fiberglass at (308)468-6178 or drop them a note at PO Box 490, Gibbon, Nebraska 68840.

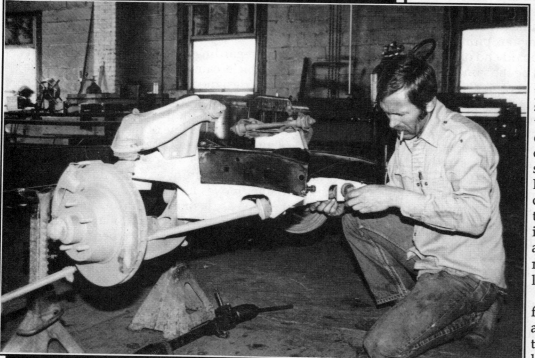

The Chrysler parallel torsion bar front end as applied to 1940 Ford with the Gibbon kit. Strut rods that run forward are shortened 6 inches. The original Ford crossmember is left in place, and a new crossmember is welded to the Ford frame.

Below-These are the components as removed from a Chrysler product. They are heavier duty than some independent front ends and work very well on most fat fendered rods. One of the major advantages is that car front end height can be adjusted with torsion bar tension.

Below-Gibbon kit ready to locate on the Ford frame. It is possible the kit will also fit other cars of the '30s and '40s.

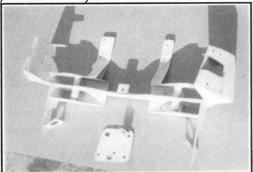

Below-The kit is designed to be used without severely trimming or removing the Ford crossmember. This adds considerably to the strength of the finished assembly.

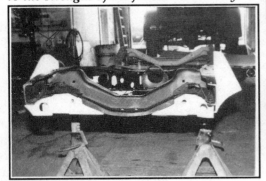

Below-Rear of torsion bars mount to a special crossmember between rails and X-member of the Ford frame.

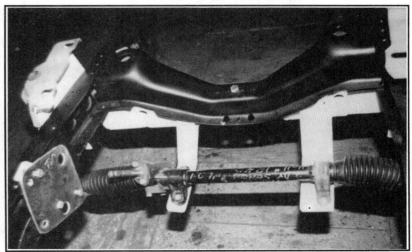

Either Saginaw cross steering can be used (mount on frame at left), or MoPar rack and pinion steering off brackets on the crossmember kit. Kit instructions give explicit story on modifications necessary.

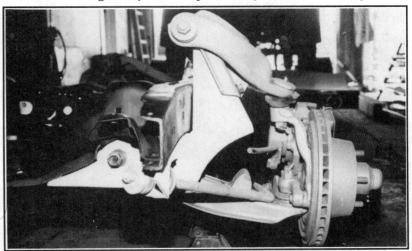

Kit crossmember is narrowed so that final wheel track width is near that of the more narrow early cars. Torsion bars give a comfortable ride.

The only trimming necessary to this 1940 Ford crossmember was the area where torsion bars pivot on lower A-arm inboard ends. Splash panels must be trimmed for clearance around upper A-arms.

FATMAN STUFF

1935 through '40

Fat Man Fabrications offers stock width (56-1/2") and 2" narrowed (54-1/2") Mustang II independent front suspension kits for Ford cars and trucks of the '35 to '40 vintage. The narrowed kit is often preferred for tire-to-fender clearance reasons. The stock width front end kit accommodates customers who prefer the Mustang II power rack and pinion steering, however the manual rack and pinion steering system has a slower ratio which makes the car easier to drive and not too hard to turn under most conditions.

To install the Mustang II kit, locate the front axle centerline by using the original axle bumpstop holes on the frame bottom. If those aren't visible, the axle centerline can be located by measuring back 11-1/8" from the center of the rear hole for the front bumper brace.

On '39 and '40 Fords, you'll want to locate the fender wishbone mount hole. It's on the front lip of the original cross-member, and is 6" ahead of the axle centerline, 4" below the frame bottom. Use the bracket supplied in those kits, welded to the Mustang II cross-member.

On all '35 to '40 Fords, save the radiator mounts when you remove the stock front crossmember. Trim them out and bolt them back in the stock location.

Use a '78 and newer midsize tilt column on cars with flat dashboards ('35 to '39), and '73 to '77 GM tilt columns on '40 Ford passenger cars with the deeper dashboard. Mount the column just like the stock column, by making or buying mounts which duplicate the original lower plate at the firewall and the dash.

Steering hookup is usually accomplished by using a splined U-joint both at the column and at the rack and pinion unit. These should be connected with a solid 3/4" shaft. This will clear rams horn exhaust manifolds on small block Chevy engine installations. For other types of exhaust manifolds, or other engines, you'll probably use the stock Mustang II intermediate shaft with its upper U-joints on top of the lefthand frame rail near the motor mount. Connect to the column with a U-joint at the column and a shaft down to the Mustang II upper U-joint. A pillow block, usually a 3/4" male rod end, will locate the shafts at the frame rail.

Shift linkage is accomplished by using the Fat Man Fabrications transmission lever and stock GM arm and rod (bent to clear the bell housing).

Mount the engine and transmission by using SAC transmount/X-member kit and the Fat Man weld-in motor mounts. If you use another motor mount kit, be sure it doesn't move the lefthand mount forward. Small block and big block Chevy engines fit easily as long as you use a TH350 automatic transmission. To install a small block Ford engine, use a '78 van oil pan and oil pickup (available from Ford), a C4 automatic transmission and an electric fan ahead of the radiator. It'll fit with no cutting. It is necessary to relocate and redrill transmission holes farther forward on the Chassis Engineering plate.

To mount the rear suspension, use one of the parallel leaf spring kits. Coilover/4-bar set ups work okay on pickup trucks and coupes, but sedans have trouble with bottoming out when the back seat is loaded. Use either a Maverick/Grenada rear axle (8" drop out, or the cover plate style) or '82 and later Monte Carlo/Malibu. Width is just right, and allows use of up to 15x8 wheels.

The Maverick/Grenada driveshaft fits Ford engines and axles. For GM powertrains and rearends, use a '78 and newer Monte Carlo/Malibu driveshaft. If the car has a GM engine/transmission and Ford rearend, use the GM driveshaft with a Ford yoke installed at the rear.

Fat Man Fabrications always uses a rear sway bar, but seldom a front bar. The nearly 50/50 weight distribution takes care of front understeer, and the rear bar is used to control body lean.

The brake system consists of ECI's kits for GM or Ford rotors on the Mustang II front end, and stock rear drum brakes. A Mustang II 15/16" bore master cyl-

inder is used in conjunction with stock '39 or '40 Ford pedal assembly and adapter. The aftermarket pedal assemblies will accept this master cylinder as is. Leverage in the pedal, along with the Mustang II master cylinder, generally provides a nice stopping effort without power assist.

1941 through '48

Fords of the '41 through '48 era all accept the same Mustang II front suspension kit, although the frames differ in body mounts (and Mercurys differ in wheelbase). 1941 Fords were built on a unique frame that requires owners to use caution when it comes to front wheel selection. These cars have narrow fenders like a '40 Ford, and Fat Man recommends a narrowed Mustang II kit. But the frame is wide like the '42 to '48 cars, which cannot accept the narrowed kit.

Recommendation is for 14x6 wheels with a centered hub. The other cars will usually accept up to a 15x7 front wheel without problems. For the axle centerline, the Mustang II kit is positioned by using the original axle bumpstop mounting hole on the bottom of the frame.

These kits can be set up for power or manual rack and pinion steering. Some people prefer the manual units even though they are a little stiffer in a parking lot. The power rack units have a tendency to leak, and there can be difficulties with pump location and nose fabrication. Some folks also think that the power units are a little too quick and light for comfortable high-

way use. Nevertheless, the choice is yours, and Fat Man Fabrications will set it up either way.

A GM tilt steering column of '73 to '77 vintage works well, mounted just like the stock column, with a fabricated top bracket and a 1/8" thick duplicate of the original lower dustplate welded to the GM column to serve as a lower mount. Connecting the shift linkage is done with the Fat Man transmission lever and GM column lever and rod (bent to clear the bell housing).

Connect the steering by using the stock Mustang II intermediate shaft in its normal position on the Mustang rack and pinion. That places the U-joint on top of the lefthand frame rail, near the motor mount. Then mount a Borgeson U-joint at the base of the column, welding in a length of 3/4" shaft to connect the Mustang II U-joint. A bearing will be needed. Fat Man normally uses a 3/4" male heim joint with jam nuts on a simple bracket welded to the frame.

Motor mounts can be either the bolt-in or weld-in variety. Chevy small block or big block engines fit easily. Ford Windsor engines fit best with a C4 auto-matic transmission that has been treated to a '78 van pan (the kit is available from Ford). Any of the available transmission mounts work fine.

A parallel leaf rear suspension system with a sway bar makes the most practical set up. The rear axle will need to have a hub-to-hub measurement of about 60". This makes it possible to use rear axles from '68 to '76 Nova/Camaro, or an 8" or 9" Mustang/Cougar rear-end from the '63 to '73 era. A narrower 8" Maverick rear axle fits nicely under '41 Fords.

Fat Man Fabrications assembles the brake system by using a Mustang II dual master cylinder with 15/16" bore diameter. A stock pedal provides enough leverage to avoid the need for a power booster, in most applications. Fat Man strongly urges the use of one of ECI's front disc brake upgrade kits. Plumb the front and rear brakes directly off the dual master cylinder, which has the proper valving for disc/drum systems.

More information about these kits can be obtained by contacting Fat Man Fabrications at 8621-C Fairview Rd., Hwy 218, Charlotte, North Carolina 28227; (704) 545-0369.

Mustang II front suspension systems are ideal for upgrading fat Ford ride, handling and braking characteristics. The unit comes in stock-width or 2-inch narrowed configurations, to suit every need.

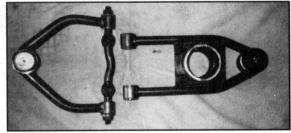

59

SPLIT WISHBONE

When Detroit originally designed fat Fords, they weren't even know as fat Fords, and nobody was looking forward to the day when folks would want to make street rods out of them. Design and engineering provided clearance for stock engines and transmissions, but who would ever have guessed that somebody might want to stuff another kind of powerplant under the hood and use another type of transmission?

Now that fat Fords are all the rage among the street rod crowd, there are often design problems that must be overcome in order to install a different drivetrain combination. The wishbone is an area of particular concern, because in its stock configuration it interferes with the installation of a later model transmission.

However, in the best tradition of hot rodding, solutions have been found to the wishbone problem. The procedure is commonly referred to as splitting the wishbone.

Pete & Jake's has a wishbone splitting kit especially designed for the '35-'40 Fords. Installation requires cutting and welding of the wishbone, as well as heating and bending of the spring perches to bring them back into alignment after spreading the wishbone at the rear. Although the kit can be installed by the skilled rod builder, less experienced folks may prefer to have some of this work done by an outside shop. These are critical components, and you don't want spring perches that are out of alignment.

Before starting this project, study these illustrations to become familiar with the differences between the axles and wishbones used in '35-'36 and '37-'40 Fords. Any of the front end combinations shown will work in any '35-'40 Ford car or pickup. There are advantages and disadvantages to each set-up.

You should be aware of several things concerning Ford and Super Bell axles, before going ahead with the project. The dimensions of a '32-'34 Ford axle are the same as a '35-'36. A Super Bell I-beam axle has the same perch bolt hole distance (36-1/2") as a '32-'36 axle. Therefore, a dropped '32-'36 Ford axle or a Super Bell axle having a 2" perch boss width will work with a '35-'36 wishbone. A dropped '32-'36 Ford axle or a Super Bell axle offers a maximum amount of drop with a minimum amount of heating and bending of the

Figure labels

Threaded end

36 3/4"

Wishbone

Center of perch bolt hole

Threaded end

Wishbone

45-degree chamfer for maximum weld penetration

Stock wishbone end

Split

Perch centerlines after split

A

A

Bend perches at points A, making centerlines parallel

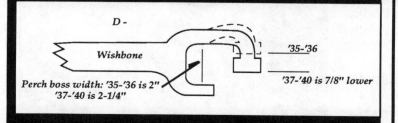

D -

Wishbone

Perch boss width: '35-'36 is 2"
'37-'40 is 2-1/4"

'35-'36

'37-'40 is 7/8" lower

spindle tie rod arms to clear the axle for turning radius. However, a dropped '37-'40 Ford axle offers very little drop and requires a maximum amount of heating and bending of the spindle tie rod arms to clear the axle for turning radius. The wishbone from a '37-'40 Ford has the spring mounts approximately 7/8" lower in relation to the axle than a '35-'36 wishbone. Perch boss width is 2" on the '35-'36 axle and 2-1/4" on the '37-'40 axle. One other thing to know is that the torsional sway stabilizer bar on '40 Fords interferes with Pete & Jake's shock kit, and the '40 stabilizer bar will not hook up if using a '32-'36 Ford axle or a Super Bell axle.

Now that we have all that straight, we can proceed with the installation of the wishbone splitting kit. After removing the wishbone from the car, cut the rear ends off 36-3/4" back from the centerline of the perch holes, as shown in the diagram. Grind a 45-degree chamfer around the end to ensure good weld penetration. Slip the threaded end into the wishbone, and square it up. Tack weld in a couple of places, then when you are satisfied that the end is square to the wishbone, weld all the way around. Allow the welded end to cool completely before installing the adjustable end.

When the wishbone is split and moved apart at the rear, the angle of the spring perches will change, throwing them out of parallel with each other. Because the perches must be parallel to each other in order to avoid shackle bind, they must be heated and bent outward to return them to parallel. Bending is accomplished by inserting a bar through the perch eye, then pulling the bar outward while heating the perch at point A (see illustration). Care must be taken not to overheat the perch eye, because it may distort. Allow the perches to cool gradually, and do not apply water to assist the cooling process.

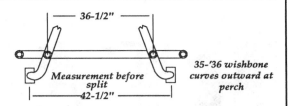

Top Views
A -
'35-'36 wishbone with '32-'36 Ford axle or Super Bell I-beam axle with 2" perch boss
Use stock width spring

36-1/2"
Measurement before split
42-1/2"
35-'36 wishbone curves outward at perch

The combination of a dropped '32-'36 Ford axle or a Super Bell I-beam axle and a '35-'36 wishbone works well when using a spring of stock width. However, stock perch width at shackle hook-up may cause tire interference with Pete & Jake's shock kit, depending upon tire size and/or wheel offset.

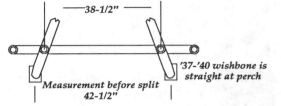

B -
'37-'40 wishbone with '37-'40 Ford axle
Use stock width spring

38-1/2"
Measurement before split 42-1/2"
'37-'40 wishbone is straight at perch

The combination of a dropped '37-'40 Ford axle and a '37-'40 wishbone works, using a spring of stock width. However, the disadvantages related to the spindle tie rod arm modifications necessary when using a dropped '37-'40 axle make this the least desirable set-up to use. Also, the stock perch width at shackle hook-up may cause tire interference with Pete & Jake's shock kit, depending upon tire size and/or wheel offset.

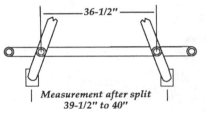

C -
'37-'40 wishbone with Super Bell I-beam axle with 2-1/2" perch boss
Use Posies Super Slide spring #35-40 SB

36-1/2"
Measurement after split 39-1/2" to 40"

This is the recommended set-up. The combination of a Super Bell I-beam axle and a '37-'40 wishbone offers the maximum amount of drop and fender clearance. Because of the narrow perch bolt hole distance (36-1/2") of the Super Bell axle, and the straight design of the '37-'40 wishbone perch, the overall width of the perches is reduced, which eliminates the possibility of a tire interference problem when using Pete & Jake's shock kit. The narrowed perch width requires the use of a narrowed spring. You can modify the stock spring by having the main leaf narrowed by a qualified spring shop, or use a Posies Super Slide spring (#35-40 SB, available from Posies, 284 W. Main St., Hummelstown, PA 17036; 717-566-3340) which is made specifically for this set-up.

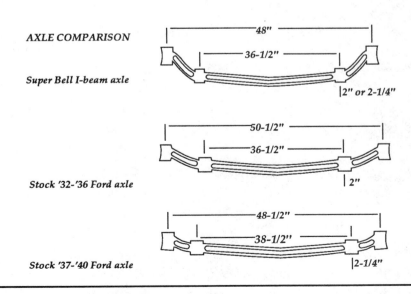

AXLE COMPARISON

Super Bell I-beam axle
48"
36-1/2"
2" or 2-1/4"

Stock '32-'36 Ford axle
50-1/2"
36-1/2"
2"

Stock '37-'40 Ford axle
48-1/2"
38-1/2"
2-1/4"

REAR SUSPENSION

The 1935-'48 Ford rear suspension consists of only two things, really. There is a cross-chassis (transverse) leaf spring, and two shock absorbers. The early shocks are of the arm type (Houdaille, pronounced Who-Die), the later types are tube (airplane) direct action.

But, almost always any discussion of the Ford suspension for these years includes the rearend as a part of the equation (although the rearend is also a separate discussion). If the original Ford rearend is to be retained, the original Ford transmission will also be used. This is possible, when using a later model OHV engine, through transmission adapters. The big problem is that the Ford transmission and rearend were not designed for the high powered output of modern engines. Transmission gears tend to fail, and axles tend to twist apart. A very careful driver can avoid these problems.

Generally, the decision is made on any fat Ford to replace the original rearend with a late model open driveline item. The Chevy Nova rearend is about the right width (measured backing plate flange to flange), as are some Chrysler products. The 9-inch Ford from modern cars is popular.

The original transverse leaf spring can be retained with an open drive rearend. Spring hangers must be made up as adapters (many rod shops suppliers have excellent kits), and some sort of axle locaters must be built to control axle wrap as well as locate the axle diagonally. It is also possible to use semi-elliptic rear springs, one on either side. Again, homemade brackets must be made, or kits installed. Finally, coilover spring/shocks are possible, again with several kits available.

It is possible to install an independent rearend and suspension, such as Jaguar XK or Corvette. There are also some rod shop built IRS units available. Most kits include a special rear crossmember, and most are very good.

No matter what rear suspension is used, the same general principle applies: Make the springing as soft as possible (and still hold the car aloft), and use firm shocks. This allows the unsprung weight to move freely. The more suspension travel room available, the better both handling and ride. It is not uncommon to see a fat Ford with little more than 2 inches of clearance between the rear axle housing and the frame. This is an effort to get the car super low. If the frame rails immediately over the axle housing are notched (C'd), additional suspension travel is possible. At least 5 inches of travel are needed for typical American highways, less than this may look zoomie, but it is inviting some harsh conditions.

LADDER BARS AND COILOVERS

An alternative rear suspension setup for '35-'40 Fords involves the installation of ladder bars. What a ladder bar rear suspension does essentially is to locate the rear axle in its fore/aft position, transfer axle torque to the frame, and prevent the rear axle housing from rotating during acceleration. With semi-elliptic leaf springs alone, hard acceleration causes the axle housing to twist, which tends to wrap the springs in an "S" shape, resulting in poor traction, and sometimes causing a broken main leaf near the spring eye. Ladder bars prevent this twisting motion from occurring, transfer this torque to the frame, and improve traction.

This type of rear suspension setup is used mainly in drag racing applications, but can also be used on the street. Ladder bars can be added to a suspension system that is set up with semi-elliptic springs or a single transverse spring. For street use, ladder bars are often employed in conjunction with coil springs or coilover shocks, and a panhard rod for locating the axle housing side-to-side beneath the frame. In this kind of application, a new rear crossmember is installed between the frame rails, and the rear coil springs or coilover shocks are mounted between this crossmember and the axle housing. A panhard rod runs laterally from a bracket on one side of the crossmember to another bracket that is welded to the axle housing, on the far side of the pumpkin.

Employing this type of suspension, the axle housing is solidly positioned fore and aft, as well as side-to-side. Housing twist is minimized during hard acceleration, and the coilover shocks/springs take care of cushioning the bumps for decent ride characteristics on the street.

Pete & Jake's offers just such a rear suspension setup, and here we have illustrations to show how the system is installed.

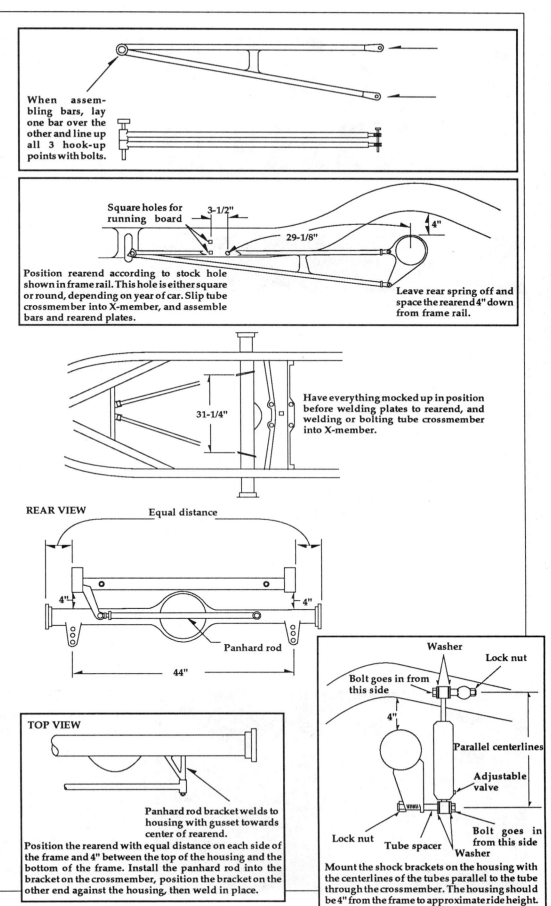

When assembling bars, lay one bar over the other and line up all 3 hook-up points with bolts.

Square holes for running board
3-1/2"
29-1/8"
4"

Position rearend according to stock hole shown in frame rail. This hole is either square or round, depending on year of car. Slip tube crossmember into X-member, and assemble bars and rearend plates.

Leave rear spring off and space the rearend 4" down from frame rail.

31-1/4"

Have everything mocked up in position before welding plates to rearend, and welding or bolting tube crossmember into X-member.

REAR VIEW   Equal distance

4"   4"

Panhard rod

44"

TOP VIEW

Panhard rod bracket welds to housing with gusset towards center of rearend.

Position the rearend with equal distance on each side of the frame and 4" between the top of the housing and the bottom of the frame. Install the panhard rod into the bracket on the crossmember, position the bracket on the other end against the housing, then weld in place.

Washer
Lock nut
Bolt goes in from this side
4"
Parallel centerlines
Adjustable valve
Lock nut
Tube spacer
Bolt goes in from this side
Washer

Mount the shock brackets on the housing with the centerlines of the tubes parallel to the tube through the crossmember. The housing should be 4" from the frame to approximate ride height.

BRAKES

by Warren Gilliland

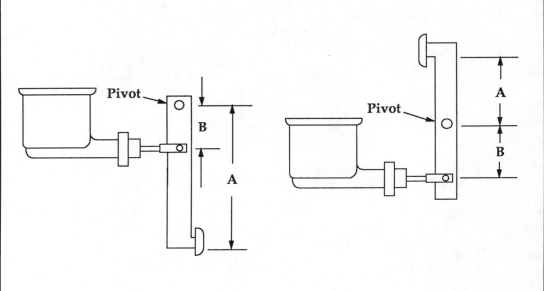

Figure 1

Because of the wide variety of Ford products currently popular for street rod conversions, they definitely constitute the biggest problem for choosing a proper brake system. Not only are there a wide variety of vehicles, there is a wide variety of weight and tire size combinations that further confuse the issue.

Since even the heaviest Ford street rod typically weighs less than 3000 pounds, the goal should be to install a brake system that will allow the vehicle to be stopped in relatively short distances, comparable to the best cars produced today. Many rodders have told me that they have learned to allow greater distances between cars because the brake system on their car was totally inadequate and they felt it was a condition that they just had to live with. Since a great deal of the pleasure of owning one of these rare and beautiful machines is the joy of driving it, anything less than a feeling of comfort and safety is an unnecessary compromise.

Being an avid street rodder, as well as a family man, has made me very aware of the importance of a safe, functional brake system. I am dismayed at the number of cars whose brake systems have inherent problems. The worst part of it is that the problems will show up a the most inopportune time, usually in a panic situation.

In order for a brake system to be truly safe, it must be capable of stopping the car under a variety of different circumstances. Most cars have brake systems that will stop the vehicle adequately from 40 mph under normal deceleration, but what happens under rapid deceleration from 65 mph or on a rainy road. Will your brake system meet the challenge of the unexpected? Do you have a car that is forever wearing out the front brakes, yet the rear lining material is like new? Does your pedal height and travel vary depending on whether the brake system is hot or cold? We will address these situations and more in this chapter, but first let's explore the system as a whole and what each component in the system really does.

BRAKE PEDAL AND MASTER CYLINDER

The brake pedal and master cylinder work together to create the system operating pressure, so we will discuss them as a unit. The master cylinder must be large enough to supply a sufficient amount of fluid to actuate all the calipers and wheel cylinders that will be feeding from it in approximately half of its available stroke, but not any more than 2/3. The second, and most often overlooked requirement of the master cylinder, is that it must have a reservoir large enough to hold reserve fluid in a sufficient amount to accommodate the displacement required when the pads wear down and the pistons move. When the linings and pads are in a totally worn state, the reservoir should still have approximately 25% of its total reserve in the tank, for a safety factor. Failure to make sure that your system meets this requirement could result in a partial or full system failure.

The brake pedal is designed for the purpose of being in a comfortable position for use, but more important, since it is a lever it must be of a proper ratio to give the best result. The pedal ratio is the reference to a comparison of the measurement from the pivot point to the master cylinder pushrod point, when compared to the measurement from the pivot point to the center of the pedal (see figure 1). If the first measurement "A" is divided into the second measurement "B", the result is the ratio. For example, in this case "A" is 3 inches and "B" is 12 inches, so the ratio calculation is 12÷3=4, which is a ratio of 4:1.

There is a formula that clearly shows the relationship of the master cylinder bore size and the pedal ratio. If you use it and plug in different values, you will be able to determine what your system is doing and whether it is in a proper proportion. (Remember, you must meet the other stated requirements for the value you use to be a valid choice). The formula is: input pressure x pedal ratio ÷ surface area of master cylinder = line pressure in psi.

Let's try the formula. Input pressure refers to the force from your foot on the pedal. Most people can develop 150 pounds with effort under a maximum braking situation. We don't want the brakes too touchy, or they will lock easily, which increases stopping distance. The ideal pedal ratio for a <u>manual</u> brake street rod is about 6:1. The surface area of the master cylinder refers to the surface area of the bore size. 7/8" diameter = .60 square inches. 1" diameter = .79 square inches. 1-1/8" diameter = 1.01 square inches.

Using the formula, 150 (input pressure) x 6 (pedal ratio) ÷ 1.01 (surface area of the 1-1/8" master cylinder) = 891 psi line pressure.

900 psi line pressure, when used to supply adequate calipers and drum brakes, will result in a proper operating effort for most cars. On heavier cars, we may want the system pressure a little higher, and on lighter cars we may want it a little lower. But the example supplied here helps us understand the relationship of the numbers.

If input pressure or pedal ratio is increased, the psi increases. If the master cylinder bore size increases, the psi drops. System pressure can be increased by decreasing the bore size of the master cylinder, but don't forget its other primary duties mentioned earlier. This is only an option if the other criteria can be met.

If a system has a problem of simply too high an effort required to make the brakes work, the entire problem may lie with developing line pressure. It doesn't make any difference how big the calipers or drum brakes are, if they don't receive sufficient pressure they will not do what they are capable of doing.

It is not only important that the master cylinder create pressure, it is also important that it relieve the pressure when the foot is taken off the brake pedal. If the master cylinder has an internal residual valve (made to operate with drum brakes), it will not release the pressure sufficiently for disc brake calipers, and a serious drag will result, causing extreme wear and overheating of the brake system. This also causes an unnecessarily high load on the drivetrain. If the brake pedal is not allowed to return all the way, it is possible that the piston inside the master will not return far enough to open the pressure compensating port (see figure 2). This would also result in serious brake drag.

Many street rods have a built in potential problem.

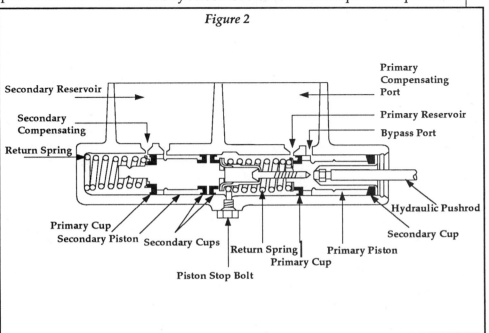

Figure 2

Secondary Reservoir

Secondary Compensating

Return Spring

Primary Compensating Port

Primary Reservoir

Bypass Port

Hydraulic Pushrod

Secondary Cup

Primary Cup
Secondary Piston   Secondary Cups   Return Spring   Primary Piston
Primary Cup

Piston Stop Bolt

Because of the lack of space (or a desire to create a cleaner appearance or use the original location), master cylinders are often placed under the floorboards of the car. This places the master cylinder below the height of the calipers and drum brake pistons, causing the fluid to attempt to drain back to the master cylinder. Since many modern master cylinders do not have an internal residual valve, this could result in a condition in which the next stroke of the brake pedal will not be able to supply enough fluid to actuate the pistons, causing a temporary brake failure. This is a potential problem if disc brakes are employed somewhere in the system. If the car has drum brakes all around and a drum brake master with an internal residual valve, there will be no problem. If an internal residual valve is not used, follow this simple rule: Install a 2-pound external in-line residual valve for disc brake calipers, and a 10-pound in-line residual valve for drum brakes. Since the drum brakes have large return springs pulling the shoes back, they are capable of overcoming the effects of a 10-pound valve and returning to their at-rest position. The disc brake caliper, however, has nothing pulling its piston back after application, and any pressure will cause it to remain applied. One final note of caution: if the master cylinder is mounted under the floor, make sure to keep the exhaust system at least a foot away from the master. Failure to do so will cause heat transfer to the fluid, bringing the fluid to a boil, resulting in potential brake failure. If the exhaust system must be run near the master, use a deflection shield or insulation material to prevent the heat transfer.

There is an abundance of street rod dealers selling the old 1-1/8" bore fruit jar master cylinder that was commonly found on Fords of the early '60s. This master cylinder, although it has sufficient volume, is not a good choice because it is only a single bore unit. In the late '60s, the tandem master was developed, which is simply two masters in one. On the old fruit jar unit, if there was an internal failure, the brake pedal went to the floor and you had no brakes. On the later tandem cylinders, if a seal goes bad it will probably only result in a loss of half of the system, allowing the car to be stopped with the other two wheels. Since the cylinders found on the later Mustang II are almost as compact, and are of tandem design, they offer a far better choice for developing a safe system.

CALIPERS

Brake calipers take the pressure in the system and turn it into force. The amount of force is determined by the size of the piston in the caliper. The larger the piston, the greater the force. For the last 20 years, Ford has manufactured two different calipers that are well suited for application to street rods. They are found on the intermediate and large Fords. In most cases, for conversion to street rods, those found on the intermediate cars are the best choice.

One of the most popular adaptations being used today for street rod conversions is the '74 - '78 Mustang II front end. Since the Mustang II had a weight (2800 pounds) similar to what a finished '30s vintage V8 sedan would have, it has become the choice of an increasing number of car builders. Several of the aftermarket front end packages are patterned after the Mustang II. Availability of both the calipers and replacement parts is good, so I rate these as the best choice for a full Ford conversion. The only exception to this would be if you intend to rod a '30s vintage Lincoln that has a stock weight of approximately 5500 pounds. Unless you intend to do some serious weight reduction of the chassis, you better start looking at the full size car components.

Many people have the mistaken impression that the size of the pad also determines the amount of brake you get. Actually, size only affects how long the pad will last. Your choice of calipers should be based solely on the piston size needed to produce the necessary force.

POWER BOOSTERS

One of the most misunderstood components is the power booster. First, since many rods have the master cylinder mounted under the floor, it is extremely difficult to fit a stock power unit in that location. To get around this problem, the novice, and sometimes professional builder as well, opts for a small aftermarket booster. This smaller booster offers a great deal less boost than the stock unit, which defeats the whole purpose of why a booster is installed in the first place. Actually, another question needs to be asked, and that is "Does this car need a booster?" The answer, in most cases, is no. Most power boosters installed on street rods are there to compensate for a mistake made in choosing the pedal ratio and master cylinder bore size. Since boosters typically run off of vacuum, they rob the engine of performance and they don't work if the engine dies. If the system is designed properly, this component is one of the first items to leave out. Of course, if the car in question is a 5500-pound Lincoln, a power booster should definitely be included in the project. If the decision is to install a booster, choose a factory unit that will do some good. The tank size does determine the amount of boost, and small tanks often provide very little assist.

DRUM BRAKES

Since the prime pieces for adaptation to the average street rod come from the local wrecking yard, the best donor cars are the '70s vintage vehicles. During these

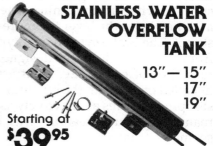

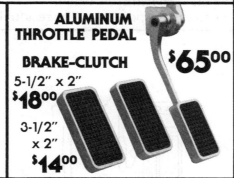

years, Ford manufactured excellent 10" and 11" drum brakes. Both of these units can be successfully incorporated into a balanced design by considering what is required to balance the brake choice for the front of the car. Also entering into this equation is the choice of tire size. The rolling radius (measurement from the center of the wheel to the ground) becomes an important factor in determining how much brake is required to stop the wheel from turning. The tire acts as a lever, and the bigger the lever the more brake it will take to stop it. The brake system on a typical production car from the factory has been designed to operate with all four tires of equal size. If larger diameter tires are installed on the rear, the rear brakes are not capable of stopping the tires as effectively as before. This is why many souped up street cars with large rear tires have so many front brake problems. If extremely small front tires are run with extremely large rear tires, it is necessary to increase the amount of rear brake planned for the car.

PLUMBING

Successfully transferring the fluid from the master cylinder to each wheel is the job of the brake lines. Most cars are plumbed with a combination of solid line and flex line. Never use more flex line than is absolutely necessary. Flex line grows under pressure, requiring more fluid movement, which makes the pedal mushy. Never use large loops, like up over the rear axle, because that makes bleeding the system difficult. For the bleeding operation to be as easy as pos-

sible, the lines must be routed so that there are no potential places for the air to be captured. It is a good rule of thumb that once the fluid leaves the master and moves downhill to a point below the caliper, the line should never again be higher than the outlet port at the caliper. If it is, the air will not move easily to the bleed screw and will require the use of a power bleeder to clear the system. Use quality steel line that is recommended for use as a brake line, and use a double flare to ensure a quality connection. Never use nylon line, as is seen on go-karts, because this type of line will fatigue over time and is much more prone to being damaged. When routing the lines, stay away from heat sources or areas that may cause damage, and always place the lines where they are least prone to being hit by rocks or other debris. Make sure the lines are tied firmly in place at least every few feet so they will not move or vibrate. Vibration can cause fatigue failure. If you are unsure how to route the lines, look at other cars or check with professionals to ensure all safety conditions are met.

BRAKE SYSTEM VALVING

Even with the perfect choices of components to achieve a well balanced system, it will still be necessary to do some fine tuning to really make the system effective under all stopping conditions. Three main valves are used in brake system balancing. They are the residual valve, metering valve, and proportioning valve.

The residual valve maintains pressure in the brake

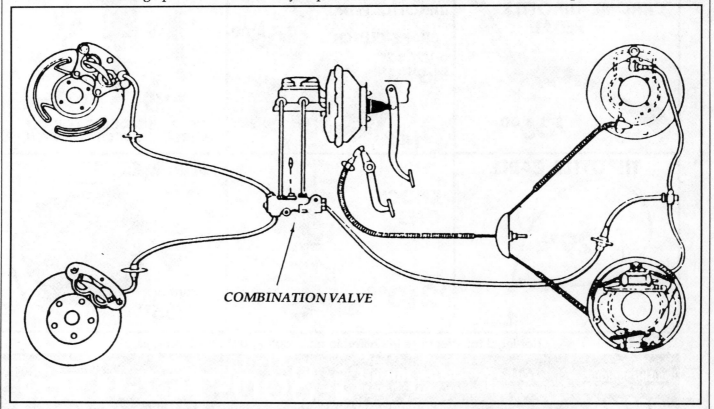

COMBINATION VALVE

line even when the brakes are not being used. This valve should always be used with drum brakes. The system requires less pedal travel when residual pressure is present, making the entire system feel firmer and react quicker to the driver. Remember, never use a residual valve with disc brakes, except when the master cylinder is lower than the caliper. Then, use only a 2-pound valve.

The metering valve is the most needed and most overlooked valve on most street rods. Its purpose is to delay the initial pressure from reaching the front calipers until the pressure is high enough to overcome the return springs on the rear drum brakes (usually about 50-100 pounds). When this valve is absent from a disc/drum combination system, the disc brakes do all of the work in stopping the car at low speeds, resulting in extremely premature wear to the pads. If you have a disc/drum combination system, this valve is necessary.

The proportioning valve is the most overused valve in the typical street rod. It has only one function and that is to limit the pressure reaching the brakes it protects. There is only one occasion that will require the installation of a proportioning valve, and that is if premature brake lockup from one of the axles is experienced. Since most street rods have large tires on the rear with 10" drum brakes, it is much more likely that the rear brakes are already inadequate for doing their fair share of the brake work. If a proportioning valve is installed in the system, a bad condition is made worse. If the valve is needed, it is best to purchase an adjustable valve that permits dialing in the amount of pressure limitation that is right for the application. Kelsey Hayes manufactures a readily available adjustable proportioning valve that is ideal for this application.

BRAKE FLUID

A hydraulic brake system will not operate without brake fluid. To a large degree, the level at which it does operate is dependent on the choice of fluid. Among other things, the more important characteristics of brake fluid are high boiling point, consistent viscosity, and good lubricating ability. All brake fluids commonly used in automobiles in the United States are regulated by the Department of Transportation (DOT). The fluid container will have a number such as DOT 3, which refers to the test designation that the fluid meets. DOT 3 and DOT 4 fluids are polyglycol base products and are hygroscopic, which means that they absorb moisture. As the amount of moisture

absorbed increases, the boiling point decreases. In a well sealed brake system, these fluids require changing approximately every 1 or 2 years, depending upon the severity of use. Since street rodders have access to master cylinders that do not have diaphragms capable of tightly sealing the brake fluid from the air, if one of these cylinders is chosen, it will be necessary to change fluid more frequently.

Never buy brake fluid by the gallon. A half used gallon of brake fluid will result in the other half of the gallon container being occupied by air. This amount of air is sufficient to cause the remaining fluid to become contaminated with an excessive amount of moisture before it is even put in the vehicle. When bleeding the brake system, never reuse any fluid

DOT Minimum Boiling Points

Dry Boiling Point	Wet Boiling Point
Dot 3 401 F	284 F
Dot 4 446 F	311 F
Dot 5 500 F	356 F

recovered from the system.

Never introduce anything other than brake fluid into the system. The seals are made from ethylene propylene rubber, which is not compatible with transmission fluid or motor oil. If either of these fluids is inadvertently placed into the system, it will be necessary to replace all of the seals in the entire system.

There is one area of caution that needs to be noted concerning DOT 3 and DOT 4 fluids. They attack paint, especially if allowed to be in contact for some time. If fluid is spilled on a painted surface, flush with water and wipe dry immediately.

DOT 5 brake fluid is more commonly known as silicone fluid. This is because it is primarily a silicone based product. It does not attack paint, and it does not absorb moisture. However, it has some characteristics that make it unacceptable for use in street driven automobiles. First, the compressibility of silicone fluid is very unstable and changes with temperature. Since the temperature of the fluid in a brake system changes under normal driving conditions, the pedal feel is affected, sometimes radially so. It is also affected by changes in atmospheric pressure (altitude). If you live in high country, don't even consider silicone brake fluid. In the racing industry, where brake systems are subjected to extreme use and temperature, it was discovered long ago to be an unacceptable fluid. Because of the expansion characteristic of the fluid, brake systems can lock up and not move until sufficient time passes for the fluid temperature to come down. Several street rodders have told me that pedals that were just fine when the car was cold became mushy after the car was driven for a while.

TESTING THE SYSTEM

The job of building a safe brake system cannot be considered complete until it has been tested and proven to perform under realistic conditions. Go to a safe area to perform some testing, subjecting the car to varying types of stops to check for feel, safety, and balanced braking under both easy deceleration and hard deceleration. Begin with easy stops from low speeds, to check pedal height and to be sure no pulling is present. Once satisfied that there are no major errors, make several stops from about 30 mph in rapid succession, to check for brake fade. It should be possible to make at least 3 stops from 30 mph with no noticeable change in the braking characteristics. Now from the same speed, attempt to make a hard deceleration and see if there is either front or rear wheel lockup. If so, the system is not yet properly balanced and needs more fine tuning. This should be checked up to full highway speed, prior to actually driving on the public streets. Never drive any highly modified car until it has been tested for handling characteristics.

On street rods, the most common out of balance problem is front brake lockup during hard stops. Normally it is because the rear brakes are too small due to the large tires. Solutions to this problem include installation of larger rear brakes, installation of larger wheel cylinders in the drums, putting smaller diameter tires on the rear, or putting larger diameter tires on the front. You may also use a proportioning valve to correct an out of balance condition, but it is wise to do as much as possible with the basic setup of the system first.

Don't forget to check the vehicle for hard deceleration from high speeds. As can be seen from the accompanying graphs, rear drum brake torque output increases rapidly at higher braking pressures and at the same time more weight is being transferred to the front wheels, which makes it easier to lock up the rear wheels. This is a potentially dangerous condition, and

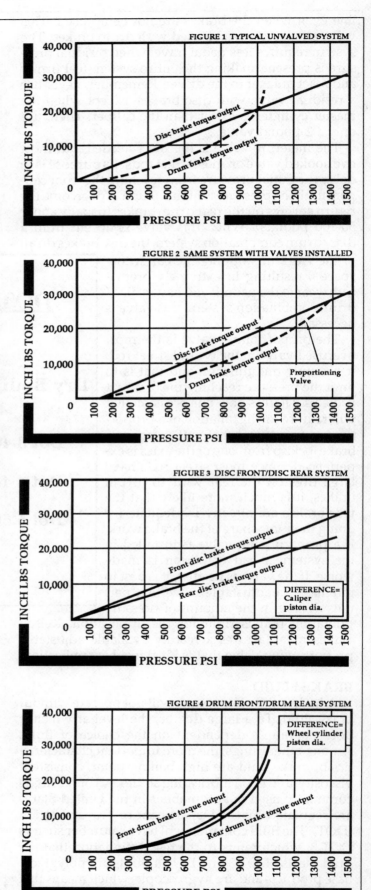

FIGURE 1 TYPICAL UNVALVED SYSTEM
Disc brake torque output
Drum brake torque output

FIGURE 2 SAME SYSTEM WITH VALVES INSTALLED
Disc brake torque output
Drum brake torque output
Proportioning Valve

FIGURE 3 DISC FRONT/DISC REAR SYSTEM
Front disc brake torque output
Rear disc brake torque output
DIFFERENCE= Caliper piston dia.

FIGURE 4 DRUM FRONT/DRUM REAR SYSTEM
DIFFERENCE= Wheel cylinder piston dia.
Front drum brake torque output
Rear drum brake torque output

is what causes a car to spin out. The single biggest reason to use a proportioning valve is if this condition exists.

Now that we have discussed the basic components of a brake system, let's take a look at some guidelines for matching these components for some of the more common Ford street rods.

T-buckets: Many owners of T-buckets like to incorporate bicycle style wheels for the front of the car. If a straight lace design is chosen, it will not be possible to install any really effective front brakes because the wheel cannot handle the load. Even with a more substantial wheel style, the suspension is very light, and single piston calipers such as the popular Airheart unit are about the only option. I consider it extremely important to have brakes on all four wheels of any car, because they provide a degree of safety. One of the more common problems with T-buckets is front end vibration during deceleration. This is usually caused when the front brakes are doing too much of the braking work compared to the rear. The front suspension is light and the excessive brake work causes chatter. If this condition exists, make sure to improve the rear braking effectiveness immediately. Don't forget the metering valve.

Since the rear tires on a T-bucket tend to be very large in diameter as well as width, the rear wheels will be the primary braking wheels. Be careful to not overbrake this type of car, because it is important that the driver have good control. Protection, in the event of an accident, is minimal.

Model A: The typical Model A will have a small block V8, 175x14 front tires and 205x15 rear tires. Choice for this type of vehicle would include front single piston Ford calipers (Mustang II variety) with Ford 10" rear drum brakes. Use a split system (tandem) master from a Mustang II. Depending on the weight bias of the car, the proportioning valve may not be necessary. Test to make sure. Stock Model A brake pedal with no power assist will supply adequate pressure. Don't forget the metering valve, or the front brakes will wear prematurely. Check the residual valve rule, since the master is under the floor. If larger tires are used on the rear, it will be necessary to go to the larger 11" drum rear brakes. In that case, on this particular car it will be necessary to use a proportioning valve on the rear brakes to protect against high speed rear wheel lockup.

Pre-War V8 Fords: Using a '35 Ford 4-door sedan as a baseline, small block V8 engine, 185x14 front tires and 225x15 rear tires, these components would make a nice system: Front disc brake components from a Mustang II, combined with Ford 11" rear brakes and a proportioning valve to limit pressure under high rates of deceleration. If tires are more

closely sized to the front, the 10" rear drum brakes should be used instead. If a pedal with a 6:1 ratio is employed, a power unit will not be needed, but a 4:1 pedal ratio would require adding a booster. Metering valve is necessary to the front brakes and residual valves will be needed if the master cylinder is under the floor. If the master is mounted on the firewall, it is still necessary to run a 10-pound valve to the rear.

1940s Vintage Ford and Lincoln: These are the heavyweight cars of the line, in some cases reaching almost 6000 pounds in stock form. The weight, and more importantly, how the weight is distributed front to rear, has much to do with what it takes to stop the car. Although I can give a good idea of what components will be needed to handle the loads, the balancing of the system will have to be done on a case by case basis. For example, a 1940 K series Lincoln limo has a stock weight of 6140 pounds. We would want to use the caliper and rotors from a full size '70s Ford or Lincoln, and the 11" rear drum system as well. Stock valving that includes metering, residual and proportion valves should be adapted from the donor car. The booster/master combination should be used or copied with regard to size. For the sake of comparison, remember that the '74 Lincoln Mark IV only weighed about 5300 pounds, so in the case of our limo we're still loading on 800 additional pounds to be stopped. I also recommend incorporating a firewall mount location for the power unit and master cylinder. Make sure to install sufficient bracing so that when the pedal is applied, the firewall doesn't flex. Check other stock automobiles for proper methods.

I have been asked if there is any benefit to installing rear disc brakes. Since rear disc brakes have a similar straight line torque output, it is easier to balance the system, and a proportioning valve is not normally necessary. But for the usual type of driving encountered by street rodders, there will be no appreciable improvement in performance. Race cars use four wheel disc brakes primarily because of fade associated with frequent hard stops and high braking temperatures that cause drum brakes to fade. Beyond that, the benefit is minimal, and the cost of the conversion could be much higher than the readily available drum components. I must admit that it does look nice, and a well planned system may allow savings on other normally needed brake components (proportioning valves and residual valves).

As a final note, please be aware that if you are designing your own car, the brake system represents the most important safety item. Do not use the vehicle until it has been thoroughly checked out for proper operation by competent mechanics. If you are ever unsure, seek reliable sources and get it right. Remember, the car in front of you may be me!

BORGESON UNIVERSAL COMPANY INC.

Borgeson offers a variety of universal joints, splined intermediate shafting, and couplers which fit almost every Mopar application. The joints can be furnished with both ends unsplined for welding and are also spot drilled for pinning, with one end splined and one end plain, or with both ends splined in any of the available sizes we offer.

We also offer "Double D" configuration (a round shaft with two parallel flats) in both the 3/4" and 1" sizes (this will fit the collapsible Chevy system).

For the serious street rodder who wants to have a "driver" as opposed to having the car trailered, we recommend the needle bearing style joint. Our joints use the same bearings as those used by General Motors.

Our splined shafting is stocked in 2" increments up to 36" in length and is very easy to measure, easy to install, safe, and removable if necessary. This allows your steering to be a bolt-together system. Our shafting is 3/4" OD which is stronger than the 5/8" OD shafting.

Borgeson universal joints have less than 1/1000" of backlash, are made exclusively for steering in high performance vehicles, and are the strongest for their size.

Borgeson offers a smaller (1-1/4" OD) non-needle bearing style joint for those who do not intend to drive their cars much or where size is restricted.

For Chrysler products, we do have six different splines as well as the 3/4" "Double D" configuration. Those who work with Mopar parts usually find little rhyme or reason to how things are done there. Therefore, we do request that you measure the OD of the shaft across the teeth of the column, box or rack and pinion. We would also need a count of the number of teeth for the application. If any teeth are missing we would need a count of half way around where there are teeth in that full semi-circle. This will enable us to accurately determine the proper spline needed.

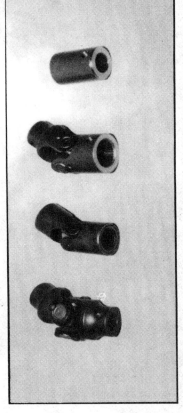

Borgeson offers a double universal joint in either style for those who have up to 60° of misalignment.

Please call Borgeson Universal Company, Inc. at (203) 482-8283 and our competent sales staff will be happy to assist you with any technical questions.

**BORGESON UNIVERSAL
COMPANY INC.**
1050 South Main Street
Torrington, CT 06790
(203) 482-8283

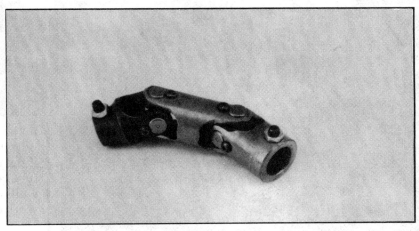

STEERING

by LeRoi Tex Smith

Directional control for any fat Ford is imperative, a fact that too many amateur builders take lightly. Too often, a very nice car is either unsafe or unpleasant to drive simply because the steering has been incorrectly installed, or poor components have been used.

So, how about the stock Ford steering gearboxes used in 1935-'48 Ford/Lincoln/Mercury chassis? As a general rule, these cross-steering gearboxes are good ... if. If they are in as-new condition. Practically none are. And, from an engineering standpoint, a 1948 gearbox is far better than a 1935 gearbox.

It is possible to get rebuild kits from antique Ford parts suppliers for some of these gearboxes. If the car gets an original type flathead engine, or one of the lighter weight modern engines, these boxes will work quite well. They do not work well if an engine that is several hundred pounds heavier is used, or if the front suspension is radically altered, or if the tire dimensions are changed, of if ... well, you get the idea.

So, start at square one. With the original Ford beam axle, the centerline of a stock type tire will intersect the pavement at almost the exact same point where a line drawn through the kingpin would intersect the pavement. This eliminates a kind of tire scrub when turning, giving a neutral steering effect caused by no offset at the tire contact point. The gearbox does not have to overcome such a problem. A stock Ford will steer lightly. Change the wheel offset, tire size, tire pressure, etc., and you alter the steering characteristics.

If a relatively narrow front tire is used, something in the neighborhood of 5 inches wide, and if the wheel is not offset much from the original, and if the original Ford hub is used, the stock Ford type gearbox (in good condition) will work rather well. A 1946-'48 box in the earlier frames will work even better. It is possible to slightly reposition these gearboxes to gain some steering shaft-to-exhaust manifold clearance, as well.

The mounting plate for the stock Ford steering gearbox is riveted to the frame. Cut the rivets and the mount can be moved fore or aft an inch or so without adverse effect on the steering. This also moves the steering shaft at the dash support, and very slightly changes the shaft/steering wheel angle. Additional clearance can be gained by flattening the steering shaft housing.

For the most part, however, contemporary fat Ford builders prefer to replace any of the 1935-'48 Ford product gearboxes with something newer and better. The overwhelming favorite is the GM Saginaw type gearbox, either power or manual. Because of this, a large number of street rod equipment suppliers market a gearbox swap plate. This is merely a flat plate that bolts to the stock Ford gearbox mount at the frame, and accepts the Saginaw box. In essence, everything remains the same, although the GM gearbox allows the use of a late model steering shaft as well. This combination usually gives more clearance in the exhaust manifold area, and the GM boxes are much stronger. Their mechanical advantage is much better, as well, allowing the use of a smaller diameter steering wheel.

The power steering Saginaw box will take up more room, and often this causes an interference with the motor mount. But this is nothing that can't be overcome. The smaller manual gearbox fits the same mounting bolt pattern. Rebuilt manual Saginaw gearboxes are now appearing on rod supplier shelves.

Other types of cross-steering gearboxes can be used, of course, such as the Chrysler types, early Mustang, Vega, and several larger import car units. The key to selection is to consider the weight and tire geometry of the donor car.

Be sure to test any gearbox to make sure that it turns in the direction you want, when mounted in the original Ford location. When the steering is turned to the right, the pitman arm (which points forward) should move to the left. It is possible to get cross-steering gearboxes that mount differently, and thus turn differently. It is also possible to change the location of the pitman arm on the gearbox sector shaft. There is often a locating feature in the pitman arm splines. This can be a double spline, etc., and a hand file eliminates the problem quickly. It is also possible to do some pitman arm interchanging, since many GM cars have arms of different shape and length.

If an independent front suspension is installed, such as the Mustang IFS, then a rack and pinion steering will be part of the new suspension. Some rodders feel that the power rack and pinion is too sensitive, too quick on the touch. Others feel that the power is just right. A general rule of thumb here is that the heavier the car, the more the power rack is needed. Unfortunately, this is one place where personal preference is the only guide.

A problem that sometimes crops up with the cross-steering is one of wheel wobble. Usually, this appears when the car reaches a certain speed, say 40 mph, and sometimes it goes away at a higher speed. Almost always, this can be traced to slop in the steering mechanism. The gearbox can be worn, the mounting can be loose, the tie rods can be worn, or the kingpins can be worn. A little bit in all of these places can help cause the problem. At the same time, especially when a dropped axle is used, it is sometimes better to set the toe-in of the tires at a toe-out stage. A little experimenting will usually show the cure. Adding a steering stabilizer (shimmy shock absorber) is not a cure.

A cross-steering gearbox is not normally relocated to change the relationship of the steering rod to the tie rod (a bump steer problem). Usually, the pitman arm is redesigned or changed because a great deal of steering rod angle can be affected by the pitman arm shape.

One area of concern that is sometimes overlooked by the amateur builder is the condition of the steering gearbox mounting plate. This place can become loose on the frame (not often), and it can be cracked (very often). This will allow the gearbox to move, and it can cause a lot of steering headaches.

Rule of thumb on any steering system: Install new tie rod ends. Don't take a chance. If you put on new ends, you know they are in good condition. You don't know a thing about the old units. You can buy offset tie rod ends, if you need some additional tie rod clearance. If you use the Heim (aircraft) type tie rod ends, be sure to use a large diameter flat washer over the outside, just in case the ends fail (and they do). The original style rod ends are much more dependable. The choice is yours.

If there is any question about building steering system components too light or heavy duty, always build too heavy. This is one area where you simply don't compromise. And, don't weld on the components. Do not weld a steering arm, or a pitman arm, or a tie rod. Leave this to a professional certified welder. Even then, it wouldn't hurt to have the piece Magnafluxed. Don't grind any of these welds to make them pretty, because you may be causing a future failure.

Finally, make sure the front suspension is checked and aligned by a professional. Misalignment can cause all kinds of steering problems.

FAT STEERING MOUNT

If you're working up a nifty '35 - '40 Ford (or a '35 - '41 Ford pickup), and want to install a late Saginaw or Vega steering box, Pete & Jake's has just what you need. It's a bolt-in steering box mount that will make the conversion fairly simple to accomplish.

Installation is fairly simple, involving the removal of the stock steering mount and bolt-in or weld-in replacement with the Pete & Jake's unit. These photos pretty well show what needs to be done.

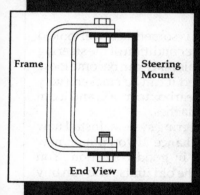

Frame | Steering Mount

End View

When viewed from the end, the upper and lower flanges of the steering mount go under the top and bottom flanges of the frame.

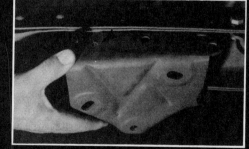

Carefully drill out and remove the four rivets that hold the stock steering mount. The mount is also held in with one spot weld (arrow) on the top flange of the frame. The weld will break loose by moving the mount in and out several times at the front. Use an adjustable wrench for additional leverage when moving the stock mount to break the weld.

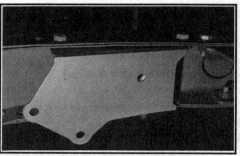

Enlarge the rivet holes to 7/16" and drill one extra hole in the top flange of the frame to match the hole in Pete & Jake's mount. Bolt the mount in place, using grade-5 fine-thread bolts and lock nuts. Make sure bolts are as tight as possible. Welding the mount to the frame is recommended, because it can move if the bolts are not tight.

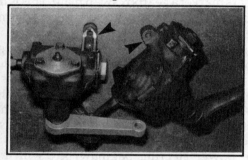

Drill out the threaded hole in the upper mounting boss on the steering box to 7/16" diameter. Grind a flat area on the back side of the upper mounting boss so the bolt head will sit flat against the box. The bolt will now go through from the opposite side. Photo shows a '70-'78 Vega and a mid-'60s Chevelle (Saginaw) steering box.

Bolt the steering box to the mount, using grade-5 coarse-thread bolts. Tube spacers go between the mount and the steering box.

Photo shows final installation of a Vega steering box, which includes Pete & Jake's Vega pitman arm (#1020) and U-joint (#1018). Panhard rod kit (#1016) eliminates lateral movement of the axle that affects steering.

ALIGNMENT

Do this on each side to the opposite rail. If the frame has measured square, this will give exact true to the rearend. Measure across the chassis from the rearend housing flange to make absolutely sure the rearend is centered under the frame. If the rearend must be moved, now is the time to do it.

Front end alignment is similar. The axle at the spindle should measure identical on a diagonal to a frame point. Adjustment at the radius rod mount(s) or the A-arm mounts will bring this into "square." Now, lay the kingpin inclination backward until there is about 5 degrees of caster in the spindle. The wishbone or 4-bar set-up can be adjusted, and shims are available to be placed between A-arm mounts and the A-arm itself. Since there are a number of different adjustments in the A-arm system, ask the front end professional for adjustment points with your particular system.

Wheel camber, or the amount the wheel leans in at the bottom versus the top, is not important at this time, although a sighting down the wheel line from in front should show the bottom tilted in slightly from the top.

If you have decent caster, and the camber is usable, then the only other factor is toe-in/toe-out. Measure across the wheels from one side to the other, using a tire sidewall or tread mid-point as reference. Generally speaking, at this early stage, something like 3/8" toe-in will work. That is, the measurement across the front of the tires will be closer together by 3/8" than measuring the same place at the rear of the tires. If you do not have a toe-in or toe-out factor in the front end, you'll feel a lot of shimmy in the steering.

Trying to measure the rear of the tires can be a problem (as in the front if there is sheetmetal in the way). A quick solution is to tape plumb bob weights to the center of the tire, front and rear, then measure from these (near the floor).

Sometimes, no amount of toe-in work seems to remove shimmy from a front end, especially one using a solid front axle. Try as much as 1/2" toe-out. This often cures the problem. Of course, shimmy can also be caused by excessive play in the kingpin bushings, or excess play in the tie rod ends. Also check the steering gearbox for wear.

A- TOTAL CASTER
Vertical
A
Forward or backward inclination of pivot pin with vertical
If top of axle tilts toward rear of car, caster is positive
Horizontal
Vertical

B- AXLE CASTER OR SLOPE OF SPRING SEAT ON AXLE
Center line of pivot pin
Forward or backward inclination of pivot pin
B
Front
Spring Seat
If "B" is greater than 90° angle, caster angle is negative
If "B" is greater than 90° angle, caster angle is positive
If spring seat slopes to the rear, axle caster is negative

C- PIVOT PIN CAMBER
Sideways inclination of pivot pin with vertical
C
Center line thru spindle
Horizontal
D
Wheel spindle camber
Degrees- angle of wheel Spindle with horizontal
"D" should equal "E"

D,E- WHEEL CAMBER
D
E
Rule
Protractor
Inches
Degrees
"E" should equal "D"

Once you have the suspension system installed, all would seem well and good. It is ... almost! Now, you must make the wheels roll true, and do what they should do in a turn.

Leave the final wheel alignment to the professional shop. However, there is a lot of alignment that you can do at home to get things at least in the ballpark. Since most projects are a long time from first movement to final driveaway, this initial alignment will help things considerably.

A note here: If you have an independent rear suspension, it is vital that this unit be aligned by the professional. Such systems have a lot to do with how the vehicle will handle, and they are not simply set with the wheels parallel to the chassis and vertical to the ground.

Rearend alignment is supposed to be right on the money if you have measured carefully when attaching all the mounting brackets. Quite often it is. But to find out, measure diagonally from the leading edge of the rearend housing at the outer brake backing plate flange, to some known point on the opposite frame rail, well forward.

THE ACKERMAN PRINCIPLE

Consider the car as it turns in a constant circle. The inside front wheel is turning a smaller-radius circle than the outside front wheel. Something must be done in the front steering mechanism to allow this to happen. This something is called the Ackerman principle, and if you look at a set of spindles you see that the steering arms on the spindles have the tie rod end holes closer to the center of the car than the kingpin holes.

If you draw a line from the center of the kingpin to the center of the rear axle, the line should pass directly through the steering arm rod end holes. If not, the car does not have perfect Ackerman effect. Current mass production technology is beginning to ignore this principle somewhat. Some new cars with rack and pinion steering ahead of the front axle centerline actually have the outer tire turning tighter than the inner wheel. Tire technology is offsetting some of this problem and so is wheel offset, but for our purposes, stick with making a pure Ackerman effect on your rod.

If it is necessary to bend a spindle steering arm for any reason, be sure and set it so that the Ackerman check line described is obtained. Sometimes, when a crossleaf spring is used on a frame with a suicide spring perch, the tie rod runs into frame interference. Rodders have cured the problem by reversing the spindles side-for-side. This puts the tie rod in front of the axle. And the Ackerman goes out the window, resulting in very poor turning control at higher speeds. If there were enough room, the spindles could be heated and bent outward so that the tie rod holes would again line up for the Ackerman check. Not really conceivable, so better to find another way and keep the tie rod behind the axle.

One method is to mount a rack and pinion steering gear directly to the solid axle. This is usually a simple matter of two sturdy brackets between the rack and pinion unit and the axle. This creates a problem with the steering shaft, however. As the axle travels up and down, the effective length of the steering shaft changes. Some new cars use spline sections in the steering shaft, and rodders cure the variable-length problem this way.

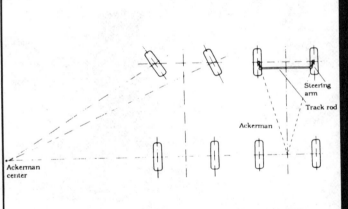

ACKERMAN PRINCIPLE/ SCRUB LINE

SCRUB LINE

One of the more important checks in any vehicle safety test would be that of the scrub line. That is, any part of the chassis/body that hangs below the wheel's diameter. Unfortunately, a large percentage of hot rod builders violate this basic safety tenet, with both early and late model vehicles.

The reason for not wanting to have anything hanging lower than the bottom wheel lip is obvious. Given a flat tire, the offending part(s) can cause serious problems. One example would be a steering pitman arm that is too low. It digs into the pavement and the car can go out of control instantly. A bracket or such grinding against the pavement sends up sparks and a fire can result.

While it is true that a flat tire seldom lets the wheel rest on the road surface, good building sense says never take chances. To check for scrub line violations, have a buddy hold the end of a long string while you hold the other end. Start by running the string between the bottom edges of the two front wheel. Then move the string diagonally from one front wheel to the opposite rear wheel. If there seems to be something hanging too low, it is worth a further check, and repair if necessary.

POWERTRAIN OVERVIEW

by Ron Ceridono

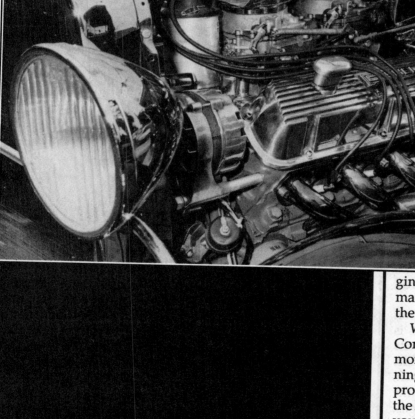

As a general rule, most hot rodders opt to replace the flathead as the source of motivation during construction a fat Ford. When the time comes to decide what the replacement engine will be, a number of things should be considered.

First, of course, is personal preference. Chrysler hemis are neat, so are J-2 Oldsmobiles and nailhead Buicks, if your tastes run toward the unusual, be prepared for some extra work. Clearance can be a problem, and everything in the way of mounts will have to be fabricated as ready-made kits will be nonexistent. But then the results can be very satisfying if you dare to be different. Lets face it, you almost expect to see a small block Chevy under the hood of a fat Ford, but the cars with something different for power are generally the ones that make people sit up and take notice.

The second factor may be what you have available. If your uncle Harry finally gives you that '49 Caddy engine that's been sitting on the garage floor for umpteen years, it may appear to be worth the trouble to install a freebie. But keep in mind, just because it's free, or you already have it does not necessarily make it a good choice. Hop-up equipment and even stock rebuild parts are scarce for some vintage engines. Parts for an "antique" or an out of the mainstream engine may end up costing more in the long run than you will save at the outset.

What you can afford is yet another issue. Consider the use of the car, and the amount of money you are willing to invest. A good running engine from a late model parts car will provide good reliable transportation. If making the local rod runs and weekend cruising is what you have planned, a used engine will suffice. If you're looking at accumulating a lot of miles, or if your performance desires call for more horsepower than stock, plan on spending more money for an engine tailored to your needs.

What fits, and the amount of energy you are willing to expend to get it in there is the final consideration. Examine your prospects carefully. A common mistake is to install an engine with oil pan, exhaust manifold, or some other type of interference, assuming parts to correct the problem can be found later. Find them first, because planning is the name of the game. When swapping engines allow plenty of clearance around the firewall and steering components. Make sure to leave adequate fan clearance, and that the carburetor mounting pad is level. Check and double check everything.

Now clearly there are reasons for all those small block Chevy powered fat Fords out there. The popularity of these engines can be attributed to a number of things. There is no other engine with a like amount of performance equipment available at reasonable prices. To make things easy there are a ton of inexpensive installation kits available that make this swap a breeze. And of course the big attraction is that the Chevrolet engine fits a fat Ford as if Henry thought it should be that way. A small block Chevy can be slipped into a Ford with no firewall or floorpan modifications. Once the stock transmission mount is removed from the Ford frame, only minor bending or trimming of the X-member is required for transmission clearance if a Turbo 350 is used. (The larger Turbo 400 or 700 require more extensive X-member modifications.) If the stock style suspension is to be retained there is adequate clearance for the original steering or Saginaw (General Motors) manual/power steering can be used. The wishbone must be split on the '35 to '40. This is only required on the '41 to '48 if an automatic is used. All things considered, it's no surprise that this Chevy/Ford amalgam is one of rodding's favorites.

Although the Chevy swap is unquestionably the easiest V8 to install, there are a number of other engine choices that can be used in a fat Ford. For the "keep it all from Dearborn crowd," there is the small block Ford. Mounts are easily fabricated, or if you would rather buy them, a number of engine installation kits are available. The firewalls of the '35 to '40 will require modification, the '41 to '48 will not. The pan must be changed to one of rear sump design and the wishbone must be split if an automatic is used. The installation of a Mustang II or similar independent front suspension using rack and pinion steering simplifies the transplanting of these engines in the '35 to to '40.

For ease of installation don't overlook the current crop of V-6s, they are compact, light and provide good economy although the performance (with the exception of turboed versions) may not be breathtaking. About the only interference problem that crops up is with the oil filter on some engines, easily remedied with a shorter filter or a remote mount.

If you elect to power your fat Ford with a Chevy, Ford, or some of the V6s, quality installation kits are available from a number of suppliers. If you decide to use something different for motive power for which no kits exist, or if you just want the satisfaction of being able to say you did it yourself, go for it. But plan ahead. Before the engine position is finalized and you fire up the welder, install everything temporarily, insure it will all fit and all clearances are sufficient. This endeavor will require creativity and above all patience. You might have to remove and replace the engine/transmission combination a number of times and it may be necessary to do some things over. But this, after all, is the nature of building hot rods. Keep in mind, if it was too easy, everybody would do it.

KEEPING A FORD A FORD
How To Tell One From Another

They say you can't tell the players without a program. Well if the players were late Ford engines, you'd need a program as thick as the average phone book.

Ford has offered something on the order of 60 different engine combinations since they ceased production of their venerable flathead in 1953. In addition to the confusion created by the wide variety of offerings, several different engines were built with the same displacement, further complicating things. If you're working with a 350 Chevrolet engine, it's a pretty straightforward issue. But if the subject is, as an example, a 351 Ford, you've got to figure out which of the three possible engines you're confronted with.

To compound the problem of figuring out what's what with ohv Fords, the same basic engine was used with varying displacements. Just as they did with the flatheads, the early Mercury ohv engines were just a larger displacement version of the Ford engine. Toss in the fact that there have been engines with cubic inch displacements of 427 and 428 in the same FE engine family (the 427 had a bore and stroke of 4.23 x 3.78, the 428 was 4.13 x 3.98), and a 429 in another engine family, and it's easy to lose track in this numbers game.

If a Ford in a Ford is what you want, the potential exists for some great combinations. But unless you are prepared for an inordinate amount of work and expense, make your decisions carefully. Building up older engines can be frustrating. Parts for some are scarce and expensive. And then the physical dimensions must be dealt with. Some of these engines are big and heavy, as in real big and heavy. Sure, you can put anything in anything, if you work at it. But unless you're just out to prove that point, use caution at this juncture.

And then there is the performance aspect. Some of the late model smaller displacement engines have much greater performance potential than their older and larger counterparts. Parts, both replacement and the aftermarket hop-up variety are readily available for the current crop of Ford engines. Not so for many of the older engines.

When it comes to putting a Ford in a Ford, the small block series lend themselves well to fat swaps, and we suggest you consider them first. Certainly others would or could work, but the hassle factor will increase dramatically. The no-substitute-for-cubic-inches crowd have managed to get the big blocks in fat Fords, but it is a tight fit requiring firewall and X-member redesigning.

To help you select a Ford for your Ford, we have compiled a list of engine series, displacements, years of production and dimensions for most of the late FoMoCo V8 engines.

ENGINE SERIES DESIGNATION

Since Ford has so many engine choices, when it becomes necessary to distinguish between them it may help you to know what Ford calls them. Some of the designations are simple, the names they are commonly called are the same that Ford uses. The Y-Block, 351 Windsor, and the FE series are examples of this.

Some of the less well known designations are as follows: 221-260-289-302 is the Fairlane series; 351C-351W/400 is the 335 series; 429/460 is the 385 series (also called the Lima).

In addition, when describing Ford engines, some will call the 351C/351M-400 (335 series) a small block, some call it a big block. We refer to it as a small block for two reasons. One, Ford Motorsport refers to them in their catalog as a small block. And two, small block

heads and 351C/351M-400 heads will interchange, the block bore spacing and headbolt pattern are the same.

Small block series of Ford engines feature an oil filter that makes the front of the engine the widest point. Shorter filters are available, or a remount mount will cure the problem. Front sump oil pans can be swapped for rear sump designs to provide necessary clearance for the fat Fords front crossmember.

SMALL BLOCK ENGINES

Small block Fords have been produced in displacements ranging from 221 cubic inches to 400 cubic inches. What confuses most folks is that Ford built three different engines with the same displacement, the 351W, the 351C, and the 351M.

First let's look at the alphabet soup. The W and C designations were used to distinguish between the first of the 351s and represented the plant in which they were built, W for Windsor, C for Cleveland. The M designation (said to stand for Modified by some, and listed as such in the Ford Motorsport catalog) was used to distinguish it from the other 351s.

Visually, the easiest way to tell a Windsor from a Cleveland or an M, is by width of the valve covers. The Cleveland/M canted valve heads have a wider valve cover, the Windsor cover is the same width as the Fairlane series (221-260-289-302). In addition the Windsor thermostat housing attaches to the intake manifold while the Cleveland/M housing attaches to the

block. (Refer to the 351M/400 description for differences between them and the 351C.)

The small block Ford in its natural habitat. Compact mounting bracketry for most accessories work just fine with fat Ford installations. The front mounted distributor is easily accessible when tune-up time comes.

DISPLACEMENTS AND YEARS PRODUCED

Years shown are for auto production, light trucks are in parentheses.

221	'62-'63
255	(underbored 302) '80-'82 cars ('81-'84 trucks)
260	'62-'65
289	'63-'68 (trucks '66-'68)
302	'68-'91 (trucks '68-'90)
351W	'69-'91 (trucks '69-'90)
351C	'70-'74
351M	'75-'79 (trucks '77-'82)
400	'71-'79 (trucks '72-'82)

BELLHOUSING BOLT PATTERNS

All 221-260 and early 289 had a 5-bolt bellhousing pattern. From mid-'65 on 289 blocks had a 6-bolt bellhousing pattern (we will refer to this as the small block pattern).

The 351W-351C have the small block bellhousing pattern while 351M/400M have the 429/460 (385 series) bellhousing pattern.

SMALL BLOCK VARIATIONS

302 BOSS

One of Ford's most famous engines, this hy-bred was produced in '69-'70 to compete in Trans Am racing. It featured canted valve heads (Cleveland style), solid lifter cam, stamped rockers with threaded adjustable studs, push rod guide plates, forged crankshaft, 4-bolt mains, special rods, and forged pistons.

351W

The 351W blocks are beefier than the 289-302, and the deck is higher so the intake manifold is unique. Bore spacing and head bolt patterns are the same, so heads interchange. Main bearing journals on the 351W crank are larger than the 289-302 (3.0" vs. 2.25"). Cams can be swapped, but the firing orders are different, and must therefore match the cam being used.

351 firing order 1-3-7-2-6-5-4-3-8
289-302 firing order 1-5-4-2-6-3-7-8

SMALL BLOCK 335 SERIES

351C (Cleveland)

This engine was only produced for four years. It featured canted valve heads that provided excellent breathing characteristics. Heads for 2V induction are open chamber with round ports, while 4V heads have a quench chamber and larger ports (aftermarket 4V manifolds are available with the 2V port size).

351C-351M/400 feature excellent breathing canted valve heads. Extended fan and pulleys make this engine look longer than it really is, but firewall modifications are usually still required.

351C COBRA JET

Appearing in 1971, it featured 4-bolt main caps. It was carried over into the '72 model year as the 351C-4V with open chamber heads.

351C BOSS

It also appeared in 1971. Again 4-bolt mains were used. Heads were 4-V quench chamber design with 302 BOSS style valve train and mechanical cam. In '72 open chamber heads were used along with pistons of flat top design. The name was changed to 351 C. H.O.

351M/400

Clevelands and M series engines are similar in appearance (they use the same canted valve head design) but there are a number of major differences. The 351M and 400 block are 1.100" taller, since this moves the heads further apart, intake manifolds will not interchange (but the heads will). Main bearing journals are larger in diameter, and the engine mounts are unique. An easy way to tell a 351C from an 351M, is to look below the thermostats. The 351C used a removable restrictor disc to control water flow. The 351M/400 has the restrictor cast in the block. The bellhousing bolt pattern is also different.

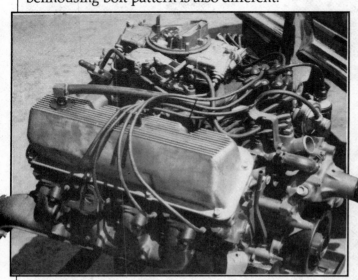

429/460 engines are big and heavy. While not lending themselves well to fat swaps, some diehard Ford fans looking for lots of cubic inches have done it.

FE SERIES
332	'58-'59 (trucks '56-'63)
352	'58-'66 (trucks '65-67)
360	destroked 390 (trucks '68-'76)
361	'58-'59 (Edsel)
390	'61-'71 (trucks '68-'76)
406	'62-'63
410	'61-'71
427	'63-'68
428	'66-'70

Bellhousing bolt pattern is FE style only.

385 SERIES (LIMA)
370	(trucks '79-'91)
429	'68-'73
460	'68-'78 (trucks '73-'91)

Bellhousing bolt pattern is 385 series, 351M/400.

Y-BLOCKS
239	'54
256	'54 [Mercury](trucks '54-'55)
272	'55-'57 (trucks '56-'58)
292	'55-'62 (trucks '58-'64)
312	'56-'60

Bellhousing bolt pattern is Y-Block only.

WEIGHTS AND MEASURES

As there are a number of water pump/pulley/fan combinations, length listed is from the transmission mounting surface to the tip of the crankshaft. Width represents the widest point of the engine (without the oil filter). Height shown is from the bottom of the pan, to the top of the rocker cover. Weight includes all accessories, less oil, fan, and bellhousing.

Engine	Length	Width	Height	Weight
Y-BLOCKS	24-1/2"	22"	23"	585 lbs
FE	27-1/2"	24"	19-1/2"	630 lbs
FAIRLANE SERIES	24"	17-1/2"	17-1/2"	460 lbs
WINDSOR	24"	18-3/4"	18-1/2"	530 lbs
CLEVELAND	25-1/2"	21"	24"	570 lbs
351M/400	25-1/2"	22"	24-3/4"	595 lbs
385	29-1/2"	24-1/2"	19"	695 lbs

OIL PANS

A major stumbling block when installing a Ford in a Ford is the front sump oil pan used on most Ford engines. The depth and location of the sump cause front crossmember interference with most installations.

The standard solution to this problem has been to change the oil pan on a small block Ford to the rear sump Bronco or 4X4 pickup unit. In recent years however, Ford has come up with additional rear sump pans that may solve the problem.

Rear sump pans for Ford engines will be found in the following applications:

302	'70 on Mustang/Capri '78 on Fairmont/Zephyr '80 on Thunderbird/Cougar, MK VII LSE Downsized LTD/Brougham
351W	'79 and on full size Fords.
351 Cleveland/351M-400	4-wheel drive pickups. The sumps on these pans are not all the way to the rear, but rather slightly forward of the rear of the block.
429-460	4-wheel drive pickups and Econolines. Again the sumps are not all the way to the rear, but slightly forward of the rear of the block.

HOW TO BUILD A BOGUS BOSS
Cleveland Heads On A Windsor Block

BOSS engines are pretty rare, and those floating around demand premium prices. There is a mystique that surrounds these particular engines, brought about no doubt by their legendary performance. Although a number of special features set the BOSS apart from standard production Ford engines, one of the most important changes can be duplicated without too much trouble.

The original BOSS 302 engines were based on the Fairlane type block and used the superior Cleveland style head for better breathing. But by making a few simple modifications to readily available Cleveland or M heads they can be installed on a 289-302 or 351W block to create what you might call a BOGUS BOSS. Granted it will lack some of the trick stuff like the forged crank and the four bolt main caps. That's the down side, the upside is that this relatively simple head swap will be good for something along the lines of a 50 horsepower increase.

To make this swap possible, a small change must be made in the heads' plumbing. The 289-302-351W engines use a front cover, and water exits the intake manifold face of the cylinder head through the intake manifold to the radiator. 351C, 351M and 400 engines do not use a front cover. The block is extended and covered with a flat plate. Water exits the combustion face of the head and into the block and then to the radiator. Windsor and Cleveland heads physically interchange but the following modifications are required due to the differences in water passages:

1. Drill a 0.800" diameter hole in the intake manifold face of the head (see illustration). Use an intake manifold gasket to locate hole.

2. Plug the square hole in cylinder head with a pipe plug, then surface heads. Install heads with Cleveland type head gaskets.

3. Use intake manifold gasket to match intake manifold.

These changes redirect the water so it will exit the heads via the intake manifold as the Windsors do.

Several shops specializing in Fords will perform these modifications to your heads, or provide modified heads on an exchange basis. One such shop is Joe Mazzie's Cars Limited/Maridyne, PO Box 666, Pleasantville, NJ 08232; (609) 646-5177. Joe also has available the components necessary to construct a BOGUS BOSS, as well a full line of Ford performance pieces.

One of the special items that will be required for this swap is a unique intake manifold. The small block Cleveland/M head combination will not allow the use of the original manifold. Two aftermarket models are available, one for the 289-302, the other for the 351W. Two versions of each model are manufactured, one for street applications, the other for race.

Pushrods are also different and must be of the longer BOSS dimensions. Pistons may be stock or aftermarket design depending on the heads used (open or closed chamber) and the compression ratio desired.

As rare as BOSS engines are, and with the performance potential that exists with them, powering a fat Ford with one seems to be a natural.

For those that want to power their Ford with a Ford, this may be the ultimate combination.

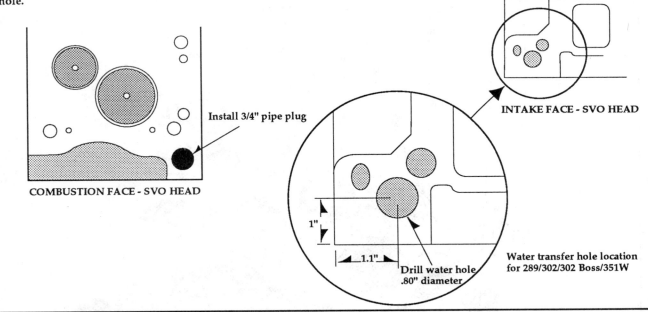

Install 3/4" pipe plug

COMBUSTION FACE - SVO HEAD

INTAKE FACE - SVO HEAD

1"

1.1"

Drill water hole .80" diameter

Water transfer hole location for 289/302/302 Boss/351W

TRANSMISSIONS
C-6

A number of transmissions have been available behind Ford V8s over the years.

The king of the hill is the C-6, a large, somewhat heavy, but bullet-proof transmission. If a high performance engine is going to be powering your fat Ford, a C-6 is an excellent choice. Its size, however, will require considerable X-member surgery.

The C-6 is available in all but early small block 5-bolt bellhousing patterns.

C-4

The C-4 is perhaps the most common of the Ford automatics. Small in size and light in weight (about 40-pounds less than a C-6), it is more than adequate to handle the demands of street use. It is available in all but the FE bellhousing bolt patterns.

AOD

The Automatic Overdrive is a 4-speed unit with overdrive in fourth. Actually, three different transmissions of this configuration are available, the A4LD, AOD, and the E4OD. The A4LD and the AOD have the small block bolt pattern, and are well suited for highway cruising. Their strength however, is suspect.

On the other hand, the E4OD is plenty strong, as it is based on the C-6. It has a low first gear, a good gear spread and overdrive in fourth, a great combination. The problem is, the thing is computer controlled and gets all its shifting information from the engine management system. If a way around that can be figured out, this transmission would be the hot setup.

FMX

These transmissions use a cast iron case and are therefore a little heavier than a C-4, and are slightly larger in size. The FMX is an update of the old Cruise-O-Matic and is adequate behind a mild street engine. It should not be considered for high-performance applications. The FMX was produced in all the various bellhousing bolt patterns.

MANUALS

Ford's top-loader series of transmissions is among the toughest of the manual boxes to be found. However there are a few drawbacks to these, or any other stick-shift transmissions. One is that clutch linkage, manual or hydraulic, will have to be fabricated, not a real big deal. The big problem is the shifter. It will require considerable remodeling of the X-member, due to its position on the transmission. Manuals often require more room than an automatic because of this. And then the shift lever, it will usually end up under the seat somewhere requiring some creative bending of the stick. Of course all these problems can be overcome if you really want to shift for yourself.

In recent years finding 4-speeds, the necessary bellhousing and attendant pieces, has become more difficult and expensive. These parts demand premium prices and are much sought after by muscle car collectors. After market scattershields, flywheel/clutch assemblies, and 5-speed transmissions are available, but the costs do add up. No doubt the lesser overall expense, greater availability and the relative ease of installation has prompted the widespread use of automatics.

"SOMETIMES WE ALL NEED A LITTLE SUPPORT"......

SMALL BLOCK FORD IN A '40

Dropping a small block Ford V8 and late model automatic transmission in a fat car can have obvious performance advantages, but there are challenges to consider. In this particular installation, overcoming difficulties at the firewall, radiator, motor mounts, and oil pan clearance all came into play.

The folks at Fat Man Fabrications did this Ford in a Ford engine swap, at the same time they were switching to a Mustang II front end. It makes for an interesting combination that results in tremendously improved performance and handling for a car that is half a century old.

Note that the support pad for '40 Ford fender brace is supplied in the Fat Man Fabrications kit.

Above-In order to allow clearance between the 302 V8 and the Mustang II front crossmember, it is necessary to change the oil pan, pump pickup tube, and its special main bearing bolt.

Below-The project is begun by installing a Chassis Engineering X-member and trans support kit, part number ES-2267. Engine and trans are moved 4-1/2 inches forward by adding a small tab on the bottom plate's forward edge. Set a piece of 1/2 inch plywood on top of the Mustang II crossmember, and move the engine/trans forward to allow about 1/2 inch of clearance between the end of the stock 302 water pump and the '40 radiator.

This particular '40 Ford was treated to a performance boost in the form of a Ford 302 cid V8 and C4 automatic transmission. Installation is clean and fairly easy, not even requiring any surgery on the firewall. Installation of the Fat Man Fabrications narrowed Mustang II front end, gives the car a nice stance as well as improved ride, handling and braking characteristics.

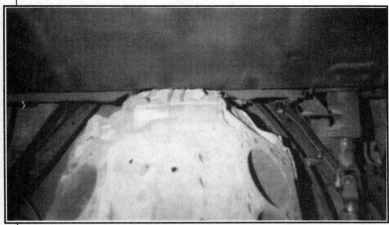

Above-Check for centering and clearance at the firewall lip, and mark position of the transmission mount bolts on the Chassis Engineering plate. Then move the transmission out of the way to drill holes, remount the trans, and then fabricate simple motor mounts.

Above right-Motor mount insulators used for this installation are '68 Ford Galaxie items with part numbers 602-11S2 NAPA.

Right-Steering hookup is easily done, using a stock Mustang II intermediate shaft that is routed to the steering column via a 3/4" rod end mount, and a Borgeson U-joint at the base of the column.

A '74 AMC Hornet tilt column with shift indicator was mounted in exactly the same position as the stock column, with fabricated 1/8-inch plate versions of the original upper and lower mountings.

Checking the initial fit indicates that the motor sits too high to allow use of a pump-mounted fan, but an electric fan mounted ahead of the radiator does the job. Mid '70s 302 Galaxie/Torino exhaust manifolds which dump between the 3rd and 4th cylinder work well. Block hugger headers are an alternative.

PUT A FORD IN A FORD

by Marian Dinwiddie

Henry never put Chevy engines in his Fords and you don't have to either. Here's how to install a Ford engine in a Ford, a 1935 Ford coupe, for instance.

Starting with the body off the frame and no engine or transmission, Gary Dinwiddie rounded up a 302 Ford V-8 Mustang engine and a Ford top-loader 4-speed tranny. The first step was to locate the engine in the frame by setting the engine in and spacing it 1/2" between front of pan and crossmember. He used an '82 Mustang GT rear-sump pan since front-sump pan wouldn't fit with a stock crossmember. The engine mount front crossmember is a piece of schedule 80 pipe that he fabricated the engine mounts on. Next, he mounted the transmission to the engine and located the transmission crossmember. By now, he was tired of fabricating stuff, so he bought a Chassis Engineering rear end mounting kit and installed it.

Now he could see the 302 would fit the engine compartment, but he'd have to cut the firewall. He measured and cut a 21-1/2" by 5-1/2" high piece out of the bottom center of the firewall. He then inset this cutout 3-5/8" back.

After getting the engine itself to fit (it took up 90% of the space), Gary's next decisions concerned finding room for necessary accessories, such as the valve covers which extended 2-1/2" into the firewall indentation. The master cylinder is attached to the firewall on the driver's side with tubing and proportioning valve, one line to the rear and two to the front brakes. Space between the top of the air cleaner to radiator tie rod is 8". Front of valve covers is 6" from front of fender and 9-1/2" inside back of front fenders. Mallory ignition is mounted on top of a modified steering pump. Battery is in the trunk, solenoid under dash. Alternator is in standard position in right front of engine. A 12" electric fan attaches to inside of radiator.

Why did Gary want a Ford in a Ford? "Because that's the way it belongs, and because everybody told me I couldn't do it."

Vent

Firewall

Cut Out

5-1/2"

3-5/8"

21-1/2"

Transmission

Cut out a 21-1/2" x 5-1/2" piece across

3-5/8" back
5-1/2" high

To make the 302 V-8 fit the underhood area of a '35 Ford coupe, a 5-1/2" by 21-1/2" piece of the firewall was cut out and recessed 3-5/8" back.

DRIVESHAFTS

You need to come up with a driveshaft to fit your hot rod, but before you head for the machine shop, do some measuring. There is a huge selection of driveshaft lengths available, and surprisingly, there is a great deal of universal joint interchangeability. For example, the Volvo universal joint is a standard Chevrolet item.

You know the type of rearend you have, and you know the type of transmission. At the transmission output shaft and at the pinion, there are yokes that secure the U-joints in place. The critical bits of information about these yokes are the measurements across the semi-circular cups that receive the U-joints. They are not all the same. With a steel tape or a set of calipers, measure carefully the distance across the yoke cup right at the edge of the machined face, to find the size of U-joint that will fit. Be aware that the transmission output shaft U-joint yoke may not be the same size as the yoke at the pinion. The ideal situation is if the yoke cups measure the same at the pinion as they do at the transmission output shaft. This way, you only need to carry one extra U-joint in the spare-parts section of your tool box, and it can fit either position.

Some U-joints are designed with all four cups the same size, while others have two different sizes of cups on the same unit. You may have larger cups for the driveshaft attachment and smaller ones for the yoke. The thing to keep in mind here is that the more unusual the U-joint, the more difficult it may be to find a replacement. If possible, design the driveshaft system to use the strongest and most commonly available components.

To determine the overall length of the driveshaft, measure the distance from the machined face of the rear of the transmission output shaft yoke to the machined face at the front of the pinion yoke. These machined faces represent the centerline points of the U-joint cups. This will get you close to the overall shaft length you need. Now shop the junkyards. Pay close attention to the U-joint sizes. If in doubt, ask what universal joint might interchange with the shaft and rearend that you have.

As you're measuring, keep in mind the splined slip joint which allows the driveshaft to lengthen and shorten as the rear suspension works up and down. Although the slip joint has a built-in travel of several inches, it should ride just about in the center of its travel when the driveshaft is installed between the transmission and rearend, and the full weight of the car is resting on the suspension. Take care to avoid inadvertently measuring the driveshaft length with the slip joint either pushed in or pulled out beyond its center of travel, otherwise you may end up with a slip joint that destroys itself when the suspension gets real active. If you are lucky, you'll find a shaft that fits. Sometimes it's a drop-in.

If you must have a shaft made, plan on paying from $60 to $150. Most communities have machine shops that can custom-make driveshafts. They will cut and fit the tube, or install a new tube (using the measurements you supply), with a yoke that will fit the rearend. Have the shaft balanced while you are at it.

Note: You do not cut a driveshaft in two and butt-weld the pieces to the length you need! This might be ok for a dune buggy, but it doesn't cut it on a street-driven vehicle.

If you are building a car with lots of horsepower, be sure to use the larger universal joints and a large diameter driveshaft tube. A good driveshaft shop will be able to advise you regarding the recommended tube diameter, U-joint size as it relates to your engine's power.

EXHAUST
SYSTEMS

by Ron Ceridono

We visited exhaust system guru Jerry Jardine for information about system components and design. Jerry recently escaped the southern California area and resettled in glorious Jackson Hole, Wyoming (right over the hill from the lavish Tex Smith Publishing headquarters). Here's what we learned from Jerry.

Headers

Headers have a definite advantage over original equipment cast iron manifolds. By connecting each cylinder to its own pipe, restriction is reduced, allowing spent gasses to be emptied from the cylinders more completely. The more thoroughly the cylinders are scavenged, the more fuel and air can go in, providing improved performance.

Manifolds are primarily designed to be compact and cost effective, usually at the expense of efficiency. The layout of most original equipment manifolds generally result in exhaust pulses that interfere with each other. The engine does not breathe as well as it could. Headers and a free flowing exhaust system are often the quickest and simplest performance improvement that can be made, according to Jerry.

V8 headers are available in two basic designs, four-tube and tri-Y. (You may have seen 180 degree oval track headers or other variations but we're going to concern ourselves with more conventional designs.)

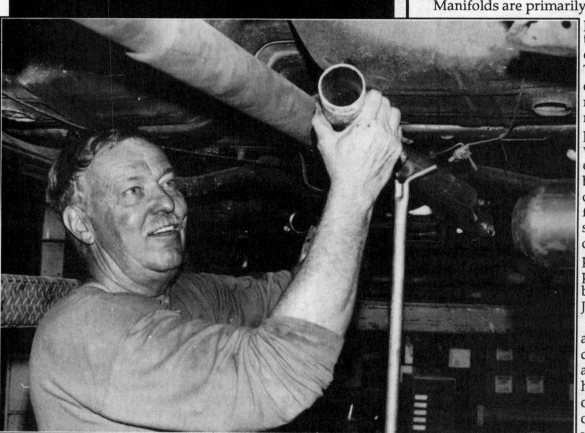

Jerry Jardine has long been the guru of performance exhaust systems. An understanding of exhaust flow dynamics and available components makes it possible for him to put together a system that dramatically improves engine performance.

Four-tube headers are just that, they use individual pipes leading to the collector. The length of the primary pipes (the pipes that go from the header flange to the collector), as well as their diameter, determine the optimum operating rpm of the exhaust system. Street headers will have 1-5/8 inch primaries, while competition versions may be 1-7/8 inch or larger. Larger primaries work best at the upper rpm range, smaller ones at lower rpm. (The often seen phrase "tuned header" refers to the adjusting of the primary pipe length and diameter to work best at a given rpm.)

It's important to understand that headers must be matched to the rest of the engine. The headers should take advantage of the operating range of the intake system, heads, and cam. If your camshaft works in the 2000 to 5500-rpm range, the headers should too. Bolt-

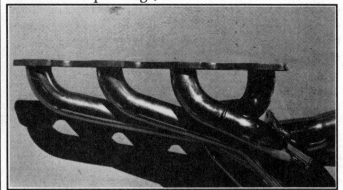

A good set of headers must have a heavy enough flange to resist warping and exhaust leakage. Quality units will have 5/16" or 3/8" thick flanges.

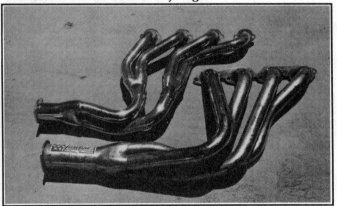

Two different types of headers are the tri-Y (left) and the four-tube styles. The tri-Y joins two sets of tubes midway to the collector, while the four-tube headers run individual tubes all the way from flange to collector.

ing a set of 2" primary sprint car headers, designed to work at 8,000 rpm, on a box-stock small block just won't work. Jerry advises that street engines that see moderate operating rpm respond best to small primaries, with large pipes after the collectors.

Generally, header manufacturers strive to maintain equal length for all four pipes. That's why the tubes don't always take the most direct path to the collector. Additional bends are used to take up pipe, the result being equal length primary pipes. From an all-out performance standpoint, ideal primary pipe length is somewhere from 32 to 38 inches. Unfortunately, there are four tubes that length, and that much pipe takes up quite a bit of space. Space is often at a premium, particularly in early cars fitted with late engines.

Finding headers to fit an unusual swap may be difficult. You may be able to locate ready-made units that will fit, but more than likely you'll have to make

your own. Kits are available from suppliers such as Headers by Ed of Minneapolis, Minnesota, to build custom systems.

The other common type of headers, tri-Ys, join pipes from two cylinders together and then run two pipes to the collector. The two cylinders that join may be different for each side of the engine, giving the headers a mismatched appearance. (Sequentially firing adjacent cylinders, such as numbers 5 and 7 on a Chevrolet, would be separated so the pulses would not interfere with each other.) Tri-Y headers are generally more compact than four-tube types, making installation less complicated. Additional clearance can mean starter removal and replacement is easier than with four-tube models. Tri-Y designs were common in the early '60s, but their popularity faded when most rodders noticed that the "race guys" were using four-tube designs. Despite the fact that they worked well on the street, they fell out of vogue, and most manufacturers dropped them from production.

Recently, several companies have reintroduced tri-Y designs. They claim this design works better than four-tubes in part-throttle mid-rpm situations, making them a good choice for highway cruising.

In recent years, tight-tuck style headers have become available and gained in popularity. These are actually four-tube style with short primary pipes. Although the short primaries are not optimum for maximum performance, they are an improvement over stock manifolds. Tony Garisto, of Sanderson Headers, feels the difference in performance between shorty style headers and tuned length designs would never be noticed on the street. He reports their research shows no measurable difference between compact design and conventional performance headers when hooked to mufflers and tailpipes.

When shopping for headers, there are several things to look for no matter what design you settle on. Quality headers will have 5/16 or 3/8-inch thick flanges to prevent warpage and annoying exhaust leaks. Tubing gauge is another area where you get what you pay for. Good headers will be made from 14 or 16 gauge material, while the cheap-o versions will be made of 18 gauge.

During installation of new headers, Jerry suggests checking to make sure the flange openings and the ports match up. If the flange opening is smaller than the ports some restriction will occur, partially defeating the purpose of the installation.

Pipes

According to Jerry, the most important part of header installation, no matter what the style, is to make the transition from the collector to the pipes leading to the mufflers as smooth and gradual as possible. He says the most common mistake is the pipe being placed too deep into the reducer, restricting the flow.

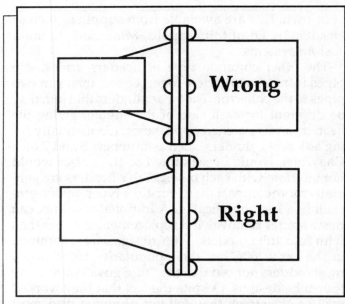

Wrong

Right

There are two different methods for bending exhaust pipes. Most common is the muffler bend, which slightly reduces pipe diameter at the bend, thus causing greater restriction. The mandrel bend is preferred for performance systems because it maintains constant pipe diameter throughout the bend.

When it comes to hooking the headers to the rest of the exhaust system, Jerry advocates the use of big pipes. He suggests 2-1/2 inches or larger. On some of his motor-home installations, he has used 3-inch pipes. He really wants his engines to be able to exhale. In addition, he advises the use of aluminized pipe. The cost is not significantly greater than mild steel, and it will last much longer.

Clearances, particularly around fuel lines, are important. Vapor-lock can be caused by fuel lines that are heated by proximity to the exhaust system. The pipes should be routed to provide as much room as possible for temperature sensitive items such as electric fuel pumps, and brake lines.   Usually, any bends that are necessary in the system are made on a hydraulic tubing bender. That works fine, but the process crushes the pipe slightly, reducing the the diameter in the area of the bend. A better method is to construct the system using mandrel bends. These

pre-shaped pieces are manufactured on a device that maintains the diameter of the pipe all the way through the arc. Building a system with mandrel bends is more labor intensive than a press bend system, due to the cutting and welding of the individual pieces, so it will be more expensive. Will you notice the difference on the street between an exhaust system constructed of mandrel bends opposed to press bends? Maybe, maybe not. But Jerry's feeling is, and we agree, all the details add up.

Balance Pipes

Balance pipes, or H pipes, fit between the head-pipes in front of the mufflers. Their purpose is to smooth out the pulses and reduce back-pressure in the system. A common misconception is that balance pipes increase the engine's power output only at low speeds. Jerry's dyno experience indicates that

A balance pipe is installed between the two exhaust pipes to reduce backpressure and equalize exhaust pulses. Sound is also affected by installation of a balance pipe, resulting in deeper, more mellow exhaust notes.

they help throughout the rpm range. An additional bonus is the change in sound that can be had when using a balance pipe. In the case of a recent project vehicle, we fired it up after installation of the system without an H pipe, (we had planned to install one, but wanted to hear it with and without). Jerry then installed a balance pipe, and we fired it up again. The difference was very noticeable. The sound was deeper and more mellow, a much nicer sound. Of course this is a subjective evaluation on our part, but we liked the low rumble with the balance pipe better than the higher pitched sound without it.

Mufflers

Mufflers are a story by themselves. We narrowed our choices down to the two most common types; reverse-flow or "turbos," and glasspacks.

Selecting a muffler sometimes has more to do with available space than anything else. Reverse-flow mufflers are short but wide, sometimes just the ticket for installations that are cramped. Glasspacks are longer, but smaller in diameter. To have adequate sound control, it is sometimes necessary to use a long

Selection of a muffler can sometimes be dictated by available space. A reverse-flow, or "turbo" muffler is shorter and wider than straight-through glasspack types. Depending upon chassis clearances, this may be just right for some cars.

glasspack, something an early chassis may not have room for.

What we have in mind is to have maximum power, with minimum ticket-getting potential. Noise control is a concern. Jerry assures us that we can have acceptable sound levels and still have adequate power.

For our project vehicle, we chose glasspacks. Jerry felt that they would perform better as they would flow more than the reverse-flow models. Two different designs of glasspacks are common — louvered core, and perforated core. Jerry prefers the perforated core, as his testing shows they have less restric-

In a reverse-flow muffler, the exhaust moves along a circuitous route back and forth until it finds the exit. This is how excessive noise is controlled.
Below-According to Jardine, a louvered-core glasspack muffler should have the louvers facing toward the rear of the car, as the flow restriction is reduced in this position.

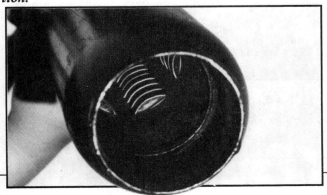

tion with little increase in sound level. If you install louvered core mufflers, Jerry advises facing the louver openings to the rear. The increase in flow is dramatic.

Muffler placement doesn't seem to affect performance, but it will change the sound. Installing the mufflers towards the rear of the system will result in a lower, deeper exhaust note. As the exhaust gasses travel down the pipe, density and pressure decrease, making the sound level easier to control with a smaller, less restrictive muffler.

Jardine prefers to use a perforated-core glasspack muffler because his testing indicates that this type of muffler offers less restriction than the louvered-core type, and little increase in sound level.

Hangers

Jerry strongly suggests the use of rubber strap isolated hangers. Although anything but high-zoot in appearance, they prevent vibration from damaging the system or transferring unwanted noise to the passenger compartment.

To get in touch with Jerry Jardine about exhaust systems and kits, contact him at P.O. Box 8488, Jackson Hole, Wyoming 83001; (307) 733-PIPE.

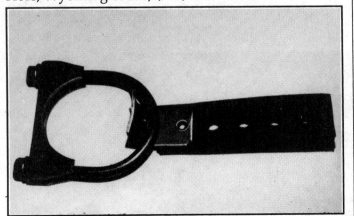

For best control of vibration from the exhaust system, a rubber strap isolated exhaust pipe hanger should be used. They may not look trick, but they are durable and do the job.

RUST REPAIR

by Leroi Tex Smith

Here is a problem all too prevalent in hot rodding today. Original flooring is rusted and must be replaced with new pieces.

New metal floorpans are available from several sources. They come with original style beads or completely flat, your preference.

Floors of older cars tend to accumulate debris and water, then eventually rust away. While fiberglass is often used as a patch, it is only a temporary fix, and the best thing to do is cut out the floor and add new metal.

Most rod builders become more involved with rust repair than with total body panel fabrication. Some inexperienced builders make the mistake of not removing all the rusted area when making repairs. If all the rot is not removed or chemically nullified, it is certain to reappear.

Where rust is really bad, it should be cut completely away and new metal fabricated. In most cases, the rust will have attacked the inner substructure as well as the outer panel, so both areas must be rebuilt. However, if only the outer skin is affected, there is no need to make a new substructure. Short term repair is possible with fiberglass, but know beforehand that this is not a cure for rust, merely a patch.

With any kind of rust repair, it is wise to chemically treat the rusted area. This can be done a number of ways. You can have the individual piece, or the entire body, dipped in rust neutralizing chemical. This is usually a part of the paint stripping process. While almost every paint stripping business will claim that there is no residual problem from the stripping, many car builders claim that the residue that gets into the body seams eventually works out and causes the paint to release. Be very careful when taking a body to the chemical vats, because when all the rust is gone there may be very little body left! This is especially a problem with cars that have intricate substructure where the body sides meet the floor pan.

Sandblasting is not a total rust treatment, simply because it only blasts clean the immediately available surface. It does not get into the crevices where the rust is. And sandblasting is only rust removal, it is not a treatment as such. Still, sandblasting is not to be ignored as a viable way to clean way rust and prepare metal. Be sure that you have a reputable professional involved with the sandblasting process, however, or do it yourself. The large professional services use equipment that can very easily warp and work-harden typical body sheetmetal if the blaster is not used carefully. Excellent home shop sandblasters are available from various magazine advertisers, and while they don't work as fast as the big pro units, if you work patiently you can do a good job.

If the sheetmetal has only a surface film of rust, such a home blaster will do an excellent job of cleaning. Heavier rust requires more effort and time. Tip: When blasting, spread a heavy plastic tarp on the ground beneath the work. This way you can save the used sand for additional blasting, and it reduces clean-up problems. Always use protective clothing and equipment when sandblasting.

Chemical rust treatments are available. None of them are absolute cures to the rust problem, but we have found Zintex (a carry-on of Fertan) to be excellent. This comes from T.C. Cowan (HC Fasteners Company) down in Texas, and it is a rust converter. Mixed with water, it will seep into every nook and cranny and kill the rust growth. After sandblasting metal, it can be coated with Zintex, and wherever the metal turns black, that's where there was rust. It's amazing how much rust residue remains after blasting or grinding. If a structure is not going to be replaced with new metal, it can be treated with the rust chemical, and in many cases fiberglass matte or cloth can be used to regain structural integrity. Zintex also serves as a kind of undercoating, and can be painted over. If air does not get to an area of rust, the rust will no longer be active. With a chemical rust converter, the chemical can be poured into all the body seams for a more permanent solution to the problem, and it doesn't seem to seep out later. A gallon of converter will usually do the average car body. Use it liberally, to make sure.

Chemical converters are not a repair, only a beginning. After the converter is used, the panel should be patched. If fiberglass is going to be used, it should be applied to both sides of the rusted area, because finishing of the panel will remove most of the glass on the outside. If fiberglass is being used to repair a rusted hole in a fender or door panel, the area should be ground clean on

Flooring can be cut away with a torch, but the new carbide wheels made especially for metal make a much better tool. It is essential to use safety goggles, and use care to keep the tool from binding and breaking.

Where the old floor overlaps onto the body substructure, drill out original spot welds. If only a small section is being installed, this can be cut and shaped at home. Larger pieces need to be commercially formed, usually.

Here, new driveshaft tunnel and side pieces have been spot welded together. This is strong enough.

These photos are courtesy of Bitchin' Products, and show some of the use of their flooring repair panels. Larger panels need stiffening beads rolled into them to prevent oil canning.

When a new firewall is being built, it is almost always necessary to create new footboards. Modern practice is to make them of metal rather than wood. They can be removable or welded in.

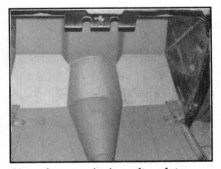

Size of transmission often determines shape and size of flooring humps. Slope of footboards will determine comfort for driver and passenger. Larger cars usually have removable footboard and center hump. Smaller rods often have everything welded to the body.

the outside before using a converter. Then the converter is applied, and then the rusted hole edges should be trimmed of "lace" and the opening perimeter should be bent inward slightly. This will allow the repair patch to get a better grip on the affected panel. Sometimes, for extra strength, a fiberglass "hair mix" can be stuffed into the hole. This will adhere to the substructure as well as the outer panes, so be cautious.

After patching with metal or fiberglass, more rust converter should be applied, just to make sure.

When working on any car, try to cut away all badly rusted substructure and replace it with new metal. This will usually be metal of about 18 gauge. You can get some of the basic bends made at the sheetmetal shop, leaving only minor shaping with hammer and dolly necessary. It is imperative that the substructure between the floor and the body be in excellent condition, and this is even more important if a new floor is being installed.

Sometimes, an older body will have had the floor and adjacent substructure removed during a channeling process. If the body is raised to original location, new substructure can be constructed. It doesn't necessarily need to be identical in cross-section to the original unit, but it should be made so that you gain maximum strength at this vital juncture. Sheetmetal can be bent to shape, or square tubing can be welded in place.

You cannot do a good job welding rusted metal. It might appear that you are getting a strong bead, but usually the weld will simply break away.

In these photos is a fat Ford with a badly rusted original floor which needed to be replaced. The procedure is not particularly difficult, and in some cases it's the only option if the car is to be saved.

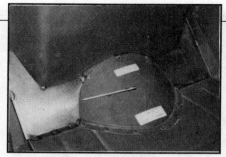

Here, the footboards and transmission hump are spot welded to the body at the sides, flooring and setback firewall. It is not necessary to make a full weld around the entire perimeter. A series of strong spot welds will work just as well.

Typical rear fender well of an older car. Sheetmetal that wraps down and under the substructure has rotted away. This is not a place for temporary fiberglass repairs. There are plenty of manufacturers now making reasonably priced wheel well replacement patch panels.

Remaining lip of the wheel well should be straightened with body hammer and dolly. Even this lip should be cut away and replaced, if it is rusted. Note the temporary body brace at rear of photo.

Replacement wheel well panel has stiffening bead rolled in place. If fenders are going to be used, attachment bolts or blind nuts should be welded in place with extra support sheetmetal.

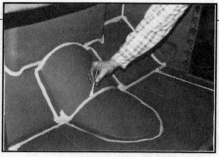

After parts are welded together, the seams should be filled with body caulking compound to prevent engine heat from getting into the cockpit. This can be done with removable boards as well. Jute, or some other kind of water resistant padding, should be used under carpets.

The rotten metal is trimmed from the body. New substructure must be bent up and welded in place, if it is rusted badly. This is an important step, as this is the foundation for the entire body.

Wheel well replacements can be deeper than stock if wanted. An extra inch makes a world of difference when wider tires are used. Edge is trimmed to fit original lip, then welded.

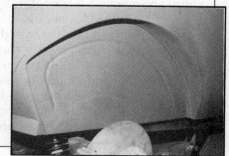

MOLDING FAT FENDERS

by Gene Winfield

Molding fenders to car bodies has been a part of rodding and customizing from the infancy of the hobby, and it is possible the procedure even influenced the Detroit auto makers.

Most of the pre-1949 American cars utilized a clamshell fender arrangement, wherein the fenders (front and rear) bolted to the body. From 1949 on, it became fashionable to have the rear achieve the same smooth appearance with bolt-on fenders, and it doesn't require a tremendous amount of bodyworking experience. Patience and a familiarity with welding is the key. Follow along with the photos, and we'll show you how we do this neat molding job in my southern California custom shop.

Perhaps one of the most common of custom treatments for pre-1949 cars has been the molding of the rear fenders to the body. The 1941-'48 Fords are excellent foundations for this work. Start by removing the fender welt and the chrome trim. The trim may or may not be retained. Tighten the fender bolts after the welting has been removed.

Grind the paint away from the welting seam, and the trim line if necessary. Get the metal perfectly clean at this stage, and clean an area well to each side of the area to be welded and filled.

Some customizers simply weld the fender to the body and then use lead or plastic filler to smooth the contour. We prefer to cut narrow strips of sheetmetal to bridge the gap. This allows us to use only a thin coating of filler.

After the metal inserts are tack welded in place, shape the metal to a concave contour. Tap the shaping hammer with another hammer for a more precise control of the shaping.

Grind the welded area thoroughly. The cleaner the metal, the better the bond of either lead or plastic filler.

Tack weld the filler pieces to the fender and body. A MIG welder from Daytona MIG works well. Sometimes we use the traditional gas torch. When using a torch, use care not to concentrate excessive heat and cause distortion.

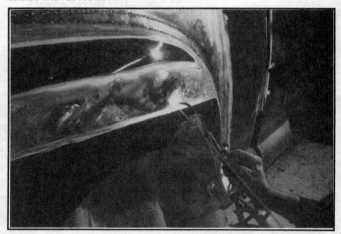

If the chrome trim is to be removed, fill the holes with weld. Some homebuilders try to cut corners by using plastic filler. We have found this not to be a satisfactory solution. If you are not a really good welder, use an asbestos base "heat dam" around the hole to reduce the distortion. Mix asbestos and antifreeze, or get the compound from Eastwood.

A small rotary file will get into the small nooks and crannies of the weld seam. Take the time to do this, for best results. Always wear safety glasses while grinding.

Only a thin coating of filler will be required. When using plastic, consult your local bodyman for the brand best suited to your region. Follow mixing and application directions explicitly.

Before the plastic filler "kicks" completely, it can be shaped with a cheese grater file.

After the filler has hardened completely, use a sanding board to get the final shape.

Right-The finished molding job requires only priming and paint, but the result is striking.

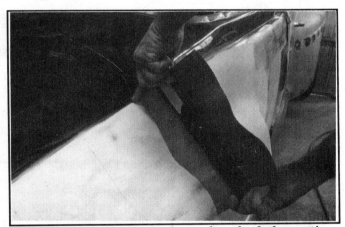

Any kind of duplicator can be used to check the continuity of the shape. Eastwood sells a good duplicator, or you can make one by drilling a series of holes in a wood base and inserting metal or plastic rods.

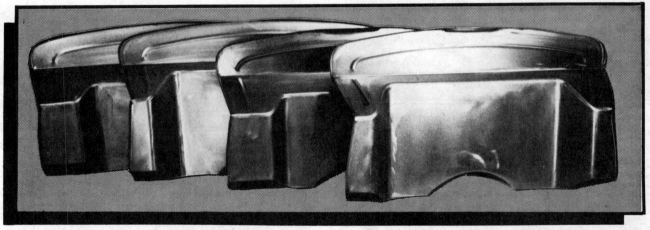
  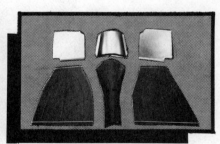

SUPER FAT

41 THRU 48 FORDS

We manufacture two firewalls for the Super Fats. One has a 1 1/4" set back and one a 4" set back. Sure you can squeeze a big block into a stocker but why run the extra weight on the front end?

Our steel floorboards are a truly modern design to convert your early body to modern drive trains. Bitchin Products has many new products for the 41/48 Ford. Below are just a few samples.

MANUFACTURER OF QUALITY PARTS FOR 28 THRU 48 FORDS

CHOPPED & STRETCHED '40 PICKUP

by Rich Johnson

When all the parts and pieces were put back together, this is what Terry Steagall's '40 Ford pickup looked like. The top has been chopped 3 inches, the cab extended 6-1/8 inches, and the hood pancaked.

If you like your classic pickup truck in stock condition, don't let Terry Steagall around it, because he has a habit of doing interesting things to vintage pickups. For instance, he built a scale downsized version of a '48 Chevy, and now he presents us with this new innovation — a chopped and stretched '40 Ford.

This pickup is due to become Terry's shop truck. He wanted to chop the top, but the tall guys at the shop would have trouble driving. So, it was decided that in order to compensate for chopping the top 3 inches, the cab should be extended a total of 6-1/8 inches to provide extra interior space.

Extending the cab 6-1/8 inches involved stretching the doors 2-1/8 inches, and moving the rear wall of the cab back another 4 inches. Even though the top was chopped 3 inches, the windshield was cut down only 2 inches. The additional inch of windshield was extended up into the front of the roof, to improve visibility for tall drivers.

The doors are hung suicide style on hidden hinges. The rear window framework was removed as a unit and the rubber lip was folded back 180 degrees, leaving the window area 1-1/2 inches larger in both directions. Tracks for a roll-up window were made and installed, so the rear glass can be opened and closed to improve ventilation.

With all the modification to the cab, Terry decided that the hood would also need some work. It was cut and sectioned to lower the front 1-1/2 inches. Functional scoops were fabricated and installed, to direct fresh air to the passengers. Fenders, hood and grille are welded together in such a way that they can tilt forward as a unit. This gives access to the engine compartment without any extra cuts or seams at the rear of the fenders.

To keep engine/exhaust heat and road noise out of the cab, Terry devised a double-skin floor and firewall. Then he sandwiched foam insulation between the inner and outer metal skins. Cool and quiet!

Power for this chopped/stretched '40 Ford pickup is derived from a healthy 331 Chrysler hemi and TH350 automatic transmission. Ride and handling are delegated to the Mustang II independent front suspension, and a Corvette rearend.

Early in the game, the doors came off and were cut in pieces. The doors will be lengthened 2-1/8 inches and then reskinned. The window frame was cut down 3 inches to accommodate the top chop.

After severing the cab's rear wall, the window area was fitted with tracks and a roll-up mechanism for the rear glass. Glass area is now 1-1/2 inches larger in each direction than stock.

At this point, the rear wall of the cab was moved back 4 inches. Trial fitting was done to see what the finished stretch-job would look like. Another 2-1/8 inches of stretch was put in the doors.

With the upper portion of the cab extended, it was necessary to also extend the cab floor.

Carefully shaped patches of sheetmetal were used to fill the 4-inch gap between the forward and rear areas of the cab. Note that the sheetmetal has been worked with a brake and English wheel to get the contours correct.

Here's how the cab looks after all the sheetmetal patches are welded together. The rear window was cut away as a unit during the top chop, and is full sized. The rear glass roll-up mechanism is in place.

Below-By using a pneumatic planishing hammer, weld seams are hammered flat, minimizing the amount of body filler that needs to be used later on to achieve a perfect finished surface.

Below-The skin has been removed from the doors for easy fabrication and installation of the hidden door hinges. These doors are hinged backward, so they open in suicide style.

Note that during the top chop and cab extension project, a length of reinforcing rod was tack welded inside the cab at the door to hold everything in alignment while the structure was apart. This is critical to getting everything to fit back together later on.

To combat heat and noise, an aluminum floorboard skin was fabricated and spaced 1 inch away from the main floor, then foam insulation was sandwiched in between. The same was done at the firewall.

Toward the end of the project, parts were trial fitted. Eventually, the front fenders, hood and grille will be welded together in a single unit that can be tilted forward for access to the engine bay.

AFTERMARKET BODIES

by Rich Johnson

Everybody dreams of sliding open the doors on an abandoned barn and finding a cherry fat Ford convertible resting under a dust covered tarp in the corner. We won't say that kind of miracle doesn't happen, but it's been a while since we heard of the last verifiable episode.

In the real world, most of us have to settle for something less pristine—maybe bits and pieces of fat bodies that have been salvaged from here and there, and painstakingly restored to usable condition. There is something to be said for this approach. It puts the builder in more intimate contact with the car. And it prolongs the building experience, thus ensuring a condition of eternally having a project to work on.

No matter how enticing these benefits may appear, some of us are less patient than eternity, and we want to get the car on the road. Because, we all know, real hot rods are driven.

Fortunately, there is a convenient option. With fat Fords enjoying a surge of popularity, the aftermarket has responded by offering a fairly complete line of brand new, rot-free bodies. And we're going to take a look at some of what's available in the way of aftermarket fat Ford bodies. In addition to what is shown here, there are other bodies available. Wescott's offers '39 and '40 Ford convertibles in several styles, and Gene Winfield is building '41-'48 coupes. (See Sources at the end of the book for address and phone numbers.) However, we regret that photos of these bodies were not available for our use by press time.

The cabriolet comes standard with swinging latched doors and rumble deck, filled cowl vent, smooth dash or dash with door and latch, garnish moldings, window channels and glass patterns.

Automotive Specialties

Fiberglass reproduction '35 and '36 bodies are available in cabriolet, club cabriolet, roadster, phaeton, and boattail styles from Mike and Kim Morris, owners of Automotive Specialties, Inc. Mike told us that it won't be long before he has a 3-window coupe available as well.

They also have parts and accessories in addition to the bodies, and the parts list in their brochure indicates that virtually everything necessary to complete a '35 or '36 is available.

For more information, contact Mike or Kim at 1050 Columbia Ave., Sunnyside, WA 98944; (509) 837-3778.

110

Standard equipment for the roadster includes swinging latched doors and rumble deck, filled cowl vent, smooth dash or dash with door and latch.

The club cabriolet body is outfitted with swinging latched doors and trunk, filled cowl vent, smooth dash or dash with door and latch, garnish moldings, window channels and glass patterns.

Below-If your desire runs to phaetons, this one comes with four swinging latched doors, filled cowl vent, smooth dash or dash with door and latch.

A boattail is something different and exciting. This model comes with standard equipment including swinging latched doors, filled cowl vent, smooth dash or dash with door and latch.

Gibbon Fiberglass

Back in '72, when Gibbon Fiberglass started business, they established a goal which was to make quality bodies that would last. To accomplish that goal, the company concentrated on choosing the best materials to begin with, building in strength to endure vibration and stress, planning in advance for the inevitable expansion and contraction, designing in reinforcement and consistent fit.

In addition to a broad line of non-fat Ford bodies, parts and accessories, Gibbon also offers three body styles that fall beneath the fat Ford umbrella. They are the '37 club cabriolet, the '37 rumble cabriolet, and the '39 convertible. Further information can be obtained by contacting Gibbon at P.O. Box 490, Gibbon, NE 68840; (308) 468-6178.

Gibbon's '37 Ford club cabriolet features a 2-3/4" chopped windshield, smoothed firewall, smoothed dash, and a fiberglass lift-off top. It is also available with front and rear fenders, smooth running boards and inner fenders.

The '37 rumble seat cabriolet features a 2-3/4" chopped windshield, lift-off top, recessed firewall, doors hung and latched, rumble hung and adjusted. The body has a complete floor, dash is installed, and all inside garnish moldings are included. Fenders, smooth running boards and inner fenders are available.

Gibbon's '39 Ford convertible comes with a 2-3/4" chopped windshield, removable top, door glass frame, interior garnish moldings, complete floor, doors hung and latched and the rumble lid hung. Also available are the fenders, smooth running boards and inner fenders. Options for all of these bodies include stock or hidden hinges, stock or recessed firewall, stock or smooth dash, and stock or filled cowl top. Note: Modifications to the body or fenders are necessary with hidden hinges.

WIRING FORDS

by Skip Readio

Ballast Bypass

Often times, especially in extremely cold weather, the starter draws too much current and there's not enough juice left fo fire the spark plugs once it passes through the ballast resistor. To compensate for this, auto manufacturers include a ballast bypass circuit in the starter solenoid.

On a FoMoCo system, the ballast bypass is on the starter solenoid. The post closest to the starter cable stud on the Ford solenoid is the ballast resistor bypass connection.

The ballast resistor bypass terminal should be connected with a 14-gauge wire to the coil, on the same post that the ballast resistor connects to. Actually, you can hook it to either the coil or the ballast resistor. You must make sure, however, that it is connected to the wire that runs between the ballast resistor and the coil.

What this does is put the full battery voltage on the points while starting the motor. Once you let go of the key and the starter disengages, the circuit opens up and you are now supplying the points with a reduced level of voltage.

For you flathead guys, that resistor in the upper inside left corner of the firewall (behind the dash) does the same thing, except for 6-volts to the weak flattie coil.

If you're having trouble starting your stocker, add a manual bypass of your own. Connect a length of wire to each of the two resistor terminals. Run them out to a toggle switch or a push button switch. A push button is preferred. When you're cranking the motor over for a long time, the resistor will heat up. The hotter it gets, the more voltage it will drop, meaning less voltage is present at the coil. Push the button, and the resistor is no longer in the circuit. You will now have full battery voltage to fire the plugs.

Ford Wiring Diagram

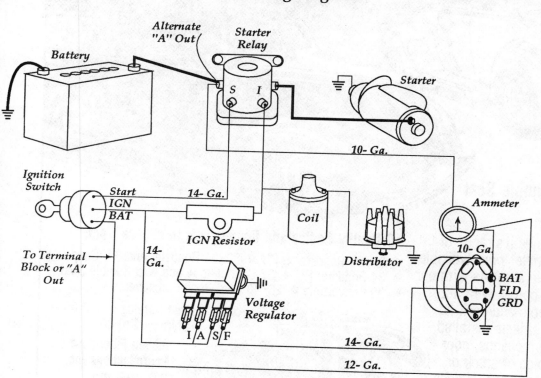

Ford Alternators and Idiot Lights

If you are using a Ford alternator and want to eliminate the idiot (indicator) light from your dashboard, there is a way to hook things up to accomplish this. Put a 500-ohm resistor across the two leads of the indicator light bulb socket when you connect the wire to the socket. In other words, run a wire to the bulb socket and the resistor from the ignition switch. Connect the other side of the resistor to the other wire on the bulb socket and connect these two to the regulator.

The "A" Circuit

In cases in which an ammeter is included in the charging circuit, the common point for tying into power for the accessories is on the alternator side of the ammeter. If an ammeter is not included in the circuit, the point for obtaining power for accessories is at the starter solenoid. We refer to these points as "A" out.

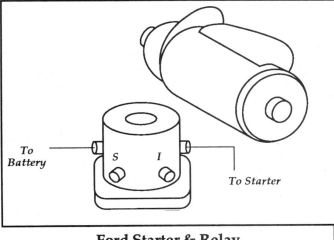

Ford Starter & Relay

Ford Alternator

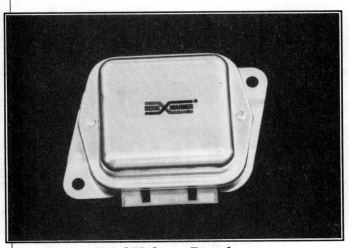

Ford Voltage Regulator

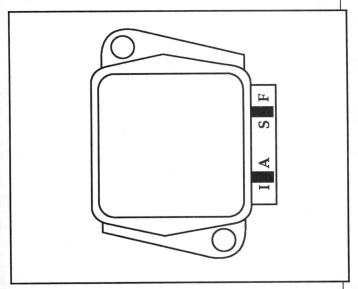

Ford Voltage Regulator

Ford Steering Column

- •(White/Blue) R.F. Turn Sig.
- •(White/Red) Emergency Flasher
- •(Green/White) L.F. Turn Sig.
- •(Green/Orange) L.R. Turn Sig.
- •(Green) Brake Light Switch
- •(Orange/Blue) R.R. Turn Sig. Brake Light
- •(Blue) Turn Signal Flasher

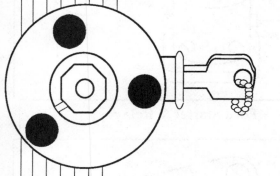

- •(Black with Green Stripe) ACC
- •(Black) To Fuse Box
- •(Brown with Purple Stipe) Solenoid
- •(White or Red with Green Stripe) To Coil
- •(Grey) Hot when Switch is on
- •(Yellow) Battery 12 Volt

Starter Solenoid

Solenoid and Starter

**The Only Company Devoted Exclusively
To Manufacturing Power Window Kits For Older Vehicles**

 **Specialty
Power
Windows**

(912) 994-9248 Technical Information
1-800-634-9801 Factory Sales Desk
1-800-728-3881 West Coast Sales (CA)
FAX (912) 994-3124

Route 2, Goodwyne Road, Forsyth, Georgia 31029

SAVING PAINT

by LeRoi Tex Smith

Having grown up in a custom body shop, I'm accustomed to people coming around wanting miracles done to their hammered custom paint jobs. Used to be, in the days of slow enamels and nitro lacquers, that mixing paint matches and getting smooth spots was just for the experts. Not so much anymore (although in this case, the fixer was indeed a pro).

I had stopped by local paint wizard Carl Brunson's body shop one day, to find him hard at work on his fat Ford coupe. This car was a really nice show quality custom, chopped top and all that sort of thing, with a very strong dark blue custom color. And Carl was right out in the middle of the trunk, sanding away.

Turns out, this heavy trophy winner was showing the signs of heavy road use. But not the ordinary type of use normally associated with customs. You see, Brunson lived several miles off the paved highway, and the gravel roads were taking a toll.

If it had been regular rock chips along the front end, the kind of traffic greetings common to any well driven car, no big deal. Except for the fact that this car was painted in a two-part contemporary paint. Even so, by mixing up a matching color, it would have been possible to dob the paint chips. In this case, however, there was gravel rash on the nose, and low on the doors and quarters, and across the deck lid.

Still, Carl didn't want to do a complete coverage, since it was right in the rod run season. Instead, he was going to save the custom paint job by doing a custom paint job. In short, a complete paint job, minus a lot of the preliminary preparation needed in normal cases. Confusing? Sort of. Just follow along and we'll show how it was accomplished.

We'll start with the last first, to show you how the finished project turned out. Note the lighter color on the rear fenders, running forward along the belt line. Although this coupe looks like a radical custom, it really is more of a mild custom without bumpers, and lends itself to being either a custom or rod.

Since much of the original custom dark blue was badly chipped by road gravel, it was decided to sand the original two-part paint (which is very hard) and apply another coat of the same color. Things started with Damon Brunson using the air sander to cut through the tough top layer of two-part clear coat. The idea is to get through the clear, and not sand all the way through the color coat beneath.

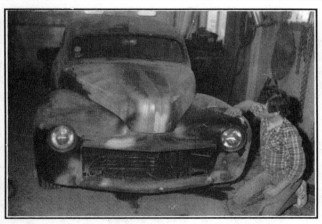

After the air sander was used for the tough work, Damon followed with hand held sandpaper, getting in all the little cracks and areas where the power sander should not be used. This is a job requiring lots of patience. 220-grit paper is normally the roughest used, followed by finer grades. The fewer scratches in the surface at this point, the less filling is required later.

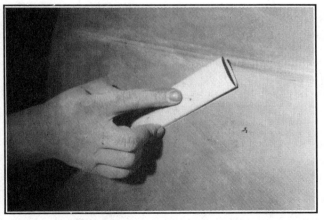

After the pits are filled, sand smooth and apply spot primer, then follow with block sanding. In small areas, it is possible to use either a traditional rubber block, or paper wrapped around a paint stick. The idea is to get the pits sanded smooth with the surrounding paint, you don't want a flat spot where every pit is. This is why the original paint is not heavily sanded (assuming that the original job was very smooth).

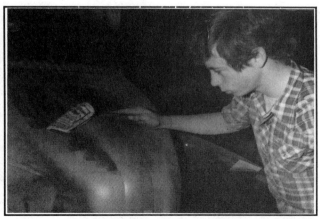

After complete sanding, the car is wiped down with a tack rag so that all the little chips and paint breaks will show. Regular chip repairing putty is then applied. Go over the entire car carefully. A second or third coat is often required to fill a pit. The key here is not to use the putty like a plastic filler, anything large will require some attention with the plastic.

Once all the pits have been filled, and covered with primer, the car can be taped off in preparation for a regular spray job. Take time here to get the tape trimmed nicely and tucked under open edges. It is far easier to take an extra couple hours taping than it is to try removing errant paint. At this point, the car should be glass smooth all over.

Left-An initial try at a new paint scheme didn't look really good, so the paint was allowed to dry, then the tape was removed, and the car sanded again, taking off the fresh paint. Another taping, and it was ready to try again.

Brunson sprays the car with a sealer. Note the front edge of the fender, where light spots show pits that have been filled. With all the excellent two-part paints now available, it is possible for even an amateur to get an excellent job. But, and this is imperative, always use the necessary protective clothing and breathing gear, and paint in a well ventilated area. Even outside painting is sometimes possible with acrylic lacquers. With most of the two-part paints, each successive coat will melt through the lower layers, giving superior adhesion.

This time, the original custom blue color came out excellent, and the new paint scheme was taped off. The biggest problem with intricate paint schemes is the amount of taping necessary. This takes considerable time, and it is best to make drawings of different paint ideas before starting on the car. All of this taping will result only in areas of near white, after the white is applied, the tape will be removed, very carefully! Pull the tape slowly back over itself, so that all edges remain perfect, and no base paint is lifted with the tape. Do not leave the tape in place after the trim color has dried.

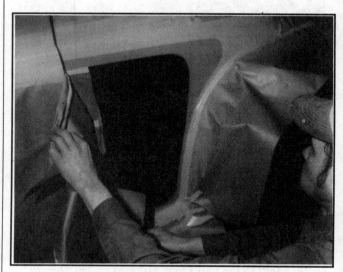

After the white trim has dried, it is taped off so that a secondary trim in silver can be applied, between the white and the base blue. Here, the tape/paper is being carefully removed. Any glitches in the paint scheme must be repaired at this time. Allow all the paint to dry very thoroughly before moving along to the next step. With most two-parts, this may be only several hours, overnight is better.

It is possible to color sand the car at this time, using 1000-grit paper, and do a power rub-out. But be extremely careful, especially around the edges of the overlay trim colors. Too much sanding or polishing can cut through the trim colors. It is necessary to feather the edges of the trim colors, removing any roughness without cutting away too much paint. A barely perceptible ridge may be felt at the edge of the trim colors, which is okay at this time.

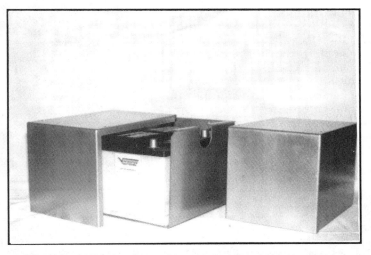

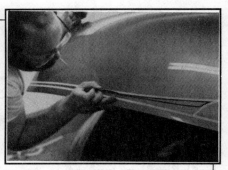

The final striping can be applied either before or after the final clear coats are sprayed. If the striping is under the clear coat, repeated polishing and waxing will not remove the stripes. Otherwise exposed stripes can be expected to wear away after several years. Here, brush artist Brooke Passey applies a wide band stripe between the white and grey trim colors, smaller fine lines can be used between the trim colors and the base blue and base silver. For the most part the pin stripers know what colors will work best. If additional color sanding and polishing of the clear coat is to be done, go slowly and do not sand through the clear. Most modern two-part paints have a heavy orange peel appearance before the heat of color sanding and polishing blends the surface.

Wrap the graphics around the door-posts and anywhere that this little extra attention will show up. The pin striping can also be pulled around the edges as well. This is one place where you will pick up lots of points with show judges.

Additional free-form striping may be in the artist's mind, and it does not have to be symmetrical. The idea is to let the overall paint scheme become a trend setter, with the striping a kind of frosting detail.

Because fat Fords tend to appear bulbous, sometimes a bit of tasteful highlight painting is enough to turn an ordinary looking custom paint job into a real eye opener. Here, note how the band of silver down the belt line (and at the door bottom) is accented with the white and further accented by the stripes.

Brunson shows off the hood latch on his car, operated from below the grille. A tiny bit of striping was added to the car's nose for effect.

And this is what Brunson's save-a-paint looked like after the final polish. By bringing the silver bustle up to the roof line, and using the side accent spears, the car seemed less bulbous (fat), and took on an entirely new character. Many rodders who knew the original paint job couldn't believe the dramatic change this scheme made. Overall time and materials was minimal, since this was not a to-the-metal paint job, but rather just a saving of the original. The car was then sold to a new owner on the East Coast. The paint scheme was done before the current craze of graphics, but even by today's standards, this is a major trend machine.

Install Authentically-Reproduced Floor Pans In Your Ford Rod and Make It An Award-Winner

The beautiful cars Ford Motor Company produced in the 30's and 40's were well-built. Bodies were structurally sound. Ford engineers, for example, wisely stamped specially-designed grooves in floors to ensure stiffening and to prevent "oilcanning". Today, however, many rod builders of Ford cars from that era are confronted with floors that, due to neglect, are rusted and must be replaced. Fiberglass patches won't do the job. To achieve a first-class, award-winning rod restoration, only floor pans reproduced to original specifications should be installed.

Toward that end, I'm pleased to offer you the products and services of my company. We manufacture replacement floor pans with all the correct grooves

Your Ford replacement floor pan manufacturing team. (from left): Phil Kiser, Bill Lankford, Paul Bradley

for Ford cars, 1935 to 1940. And, exactly like original, the pans are made with the finest 18 gauge (.047 thick) cold rolled steel. Our state-of-the-art stamping machinery produces maximum sharpness of detail and accuracy in size that assures good fit and easier welding.

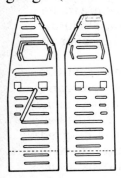
1935-36 Ford Car Floor Pan Configuration

Pans are made for Ford Tudor and Fordor models, coupes, roadsters, cabriolets, phaetons and station wagons. They are made in both full units and as separated sections and can be purchased either way. Front and rear sections are cut to the full width of body dimensions, thus providing sufficient metal for bending up along the driveshaft tunnel and sides. We do not manufacture nor do we supply driveshaft tunnels.

In addition to floor pans, we manufacture special sections as a rumble seat riser and trunk floor for

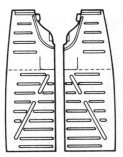
1937-38 Ford Car Floor Pan Configuration

Using original body parts as prototypes, Bill Lankford designs dies to reproduce pans to exact original patterns.

1935-1936 roadsters and cabriolets and a trunk floor for the 1940 Ford opera coupe.

If you are a knowledgeable welder or have a good welding source, installation of our floor pans can be accomplished easily. After cutting out the rusty floors and grinding away rough edges, the new floor sections are welded in place. And the job can be done with the body on or off the chassis.

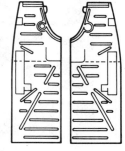
1939-40 Ford Car Floor Pan Configuration

We have served over 2000 antique Ford car enthusiasts in the United States, Canada, Europe, South America and Australia. Underneath all of the glamour of many of the beautifully restored '35 to '40 Fords proudly displayed at rod and car shows, our floor pans are quietly and effectively doing their job in helping to win awards. We'd like to help you too. Call or write today. Ask for our brochure featuring floor pan dimensions, installation pointers and prices. We accept phone orders for immediate shipment.

Phone: 704-392-3206
4200 South I-85
Charlotte, North Carolina, 28214

123

A CASE IN POINT

1935 FORD SEDAN CONVERTIBLE

by LeRoi Tex Smith

There are two kinds of Fat Fords (other than finished and unfinished). There are the Regular Fats, 1935-1940, and the Ultra Fats, 1941-48. The ultra's seem to be a tad more rotund than the regular versions. Interestingly, there is tremendous similarity between them all.

What we cover here on my old 1935 four-door sedan convert will apply to nearly all fat Fords. Yes, the body is different, but not a lot. Yes, there is far more wood in this car than in most Fords. No big deal. Overall, what I have done to this car is required of all fat Ford projects. In fact, I am gathering parts right now for another convert sedan project, a 1947 Ford Tudor that will use a modified Chevelle frame, 1948 Ford convert doors/cowl/quarter section, and a Carson-style top. It will build very much like this project.

I got this car back in 1972, in answer to a magazine wanted ad. I wanted a phaeton, none showed up. This one was in Douglas, Wyoming, at a keen price of two 1934 Ford bumpers. But, it was a sedan convertible and it was in marginal shape. The restorers wouldn't even look at it. Obviously, a perfect street rod start.

All that I had for a start was a body, badly damaged, and a frame. I scrounged a hood and fenders. Although the 1936 fenders/hood/grille will fit a 1935 body, there is a slight difference in fenders and a big difference in grille. I wanted to stay 1935 to be more hot rod than custom.

In this case, the car was to be built following the home-grown formula as much as possible. I wanted to keep the costs reasonable, and do most of the work myself. First order of business was to remove the body from the frame, and start from scratch. If the body had been in better shape, first thing done would have been bracing between all doors, fore-aft and laterally. Any time an open body is removed from a frame, the body does strange things to future re-alignment. Closed bodies offer no such problems.

Although fat Fords may seem like "new" cars, they are really more than 4 decades old. Nowhere will this age show more than in the frame, especially in the rust-belt states. Although all fat Fords have a doubled frame (two pieces of metal in critical strength areas), most of them will fall victim to rust, especially between the frame layers and at body mount pads (which usually rivet to the frame). There are a few frame repair pieces available from mail-order suppliers, or you can make up

The beginning of this, or any fat Ford project that includes work on the frame, starts with checking the frame for square. Measure diagonally across the frame from several different points, check this measurement with an opposite side measurement. The factory normally considered 1/8-inch tolerance acceptable. While this will show if the frame is bent out of square, it will not readily show a twist. Work from a flat surface and measure upward to similar points of the frame to determine any twist, bow or sag.

your own just as well. And you can pirate good pieces from other frames as substitutes. Refer to our frame drawings and note that the general shape/design of all fat Ford frames are similar. Only the measurements change. That means some interchangeability is possible, relative to parts.

After going over the frame carefully, welding cracks and substituting parts, I sandblasted it thoroughly. Small imperfections got a very thin filler of plastic, even though when covered by a body nothing could really be seen. A two-part Deltron paint was used on the frame. There are lots of modifications to this particular frame, so follow along with the photos to see what happened.

At first, I was going to use a dropped Super Bell axle, with disc brakes and early Ford front spindles. Out back, a Chevy rearend was used. A couple of years into the project (and a move to Dallas), I decided that perhaps I would go with a Mustang independent front suspension. Gene Reese happened to have a shop in the area, and was a master at making such changes, so we did the job in about a day using his frame table. Why change? Mostly because I wanted to work up an IFS at the front and see if it would improve the ride on the longer wheelbase fat Fords. I've ridden in a number of similar swaps. Frankly, if the original Ford style cross-leaf spring setup and steering gear are set up correctly, it is difficult to note a difference. The real test comes on certain older concrete roads, those that have uneven cement blocks that cause shorter wheelbase Ford suspended cars to buck. An IFS (front or rear) cures this problem for the most part.

Bodywork on this particular car was unusual, in that the rear fender inner panels had been cut out, and the car (as a custom built item from the factory) used a great deal of body wood. I cured the fender panels by installing modified sedan units. Bad wood was cured by making new wood, and using a product called Kwik-Poly for minor repairs (24 St. Henry Ct, St. Charles, MO 63301).

In nearly every way, this particular project could be called a total reconstruction. The frame and suspension were pretty much straightforward hot rodding, but the body called for some extensive and innovate restoration techniques. All of this took up the better part of 4 years of spare time building. Just as I got to the point where all the parts were fitting well and I could see light at the tunnel end, I sold the car to John Rutledge. Back to southern California it went, for another resting period before final construction.

John got back on the project late in 1990, and we will have a total update on his finishes and changes in a forthcoming issue of Hot Rod Mechanix.

Check through what we did on this car. Almost everything applies to virtually all fat Fords. There are probably some ideas you can use.

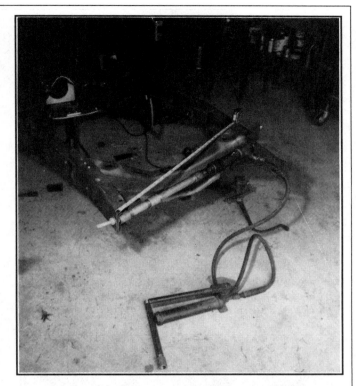

A hydraulic jack (or a very large manual jack) can be used to straighten the frame. Here, the front frame horns were bent slightly and were brought back to 1/16-inch tolerance.

Most older Ford frames will show some damage, especially those that lived life on the farm. Here, the spreader between frame side rail and X-member has been thrashed by stumps, rocks, etc. Some open Fords may have additional supports. Mostly, these braces keep the rails from rolling (twisting).

125

Straighten the original braces, scrounge good braces from other frames, or even make up new units. Sheet stock can be used to create braces, or tubing can be made into braces.

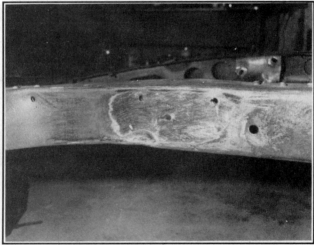

If there is an exposed section of frame that is badly dented and cannot be completely straightened, fill with lead. Do not rely on a thick coating of plastic filler. Keep heat from a torch minimal, since the frame will warp just like a lighter gauge metal.

In rustbelt areas, expect older Ford frames to pit badly along the top lip, and the sides where the body drops over the frame slightly. Usually, such frames also have badly rusted body support perches (the brackets that are riveted to the frame rail sides). Replace these perches by making new units, repair rusted sections of frame (late model pickup trucks have channel frame rails that work well for replacement pieces). Always sandblast a frame to get a really good assessment of rust damage. Pay particular attention to areas of frame where the X-member continues inside the rails for a double layer.

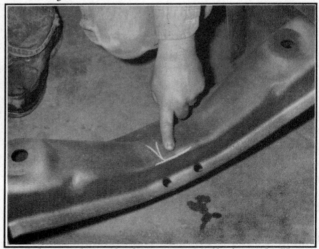

Look for cracks in the frame, especially from the X-member forward (the engine area) and around the front crossmember. Here, the frame was cracked where U-bolts had pulled too tight. Weld thoroughly, and keep in mind that if too much weld bead is removed by grinding, the area will again be weakened.

Left-If the original Ford transmission is going to be re-tained, no work at the X-member center section will be necessary. However, most all modern hot rods use some kind of late model OHV engine and modern transmission. This means the very backbone of the Ford frame must be removed, the saddle between X-member rails. Cut out the rivets, but be sure the frame is solidly supported at several points on side rails, and under the X-member rails.

You can make up a new saddle to fit the X-member. In this case, a replacement from Chassis Engineering was included. This kit is designed to bolt to existing rivet holes, with the large flat plate on the bottom, the humped plate on top, and the U-shape insert between. In some cases, depending upon the modern transmission used, it is necessary to cut the X-member rails at the closest approach and insert straight sections of rail (for more trans clearance). Again, there are some aftermarket kits, but pieces of late model pickup frame work just fine for inserts.

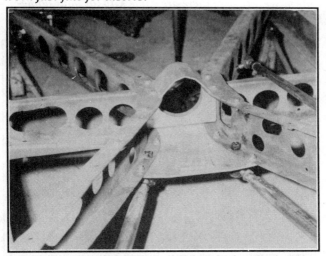

The original Ford wishbone pivoted at the exact center-line of the X-member. With a modern engine/transmission combo, this wishbone usually has a clearance problem with the transmission (especially automatics). If the stock Ford type beam or tube front axle is retained, the wishbone must normally be split as shown, or a 4-bar axle locating system used. When the wishbone is split only a small amount, as shown, very little front axle "stack" results. The Chassis Engineering X-member saddle kit takes this into account.

Right-The lower plate includes some tapered spuds for the wishbone ends. Remember that Ford tie rod ends have a different taper than GM rod ends. Taper reams can be purchased from auto parts stores. The Ford taper usually requires a special order, however.

The existing rivet holes need to be enlarged slightly, and this will also give better alignment with the Chassis Engineering kit pieces for the frame saddle.

Whether using a kit X-member center section replacement, or making your own, it usually works best to fit everything with bolts first.

The original Ford wishbone used a ball pivot. Here, it has been cut from the wishbone tubes. Threaded inserts are welded into the tubes, heavy duty tie rod ends are used. After the car is assembled, be sure and have a professional set up the front end alignment. On a beam Ford axle, caster will probably be 5 degrees on the driver's side, 5-1/2 degrees on passenger side. It may go as high as 7 degrees to get the car to handle smoothly.

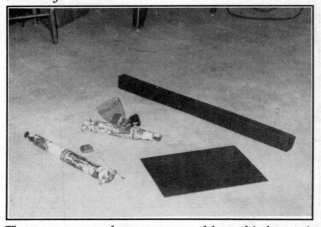

The rear crossmember was removed from this frame. A piece of heavy wall 2x3-inch rectangular tubing was substituted.

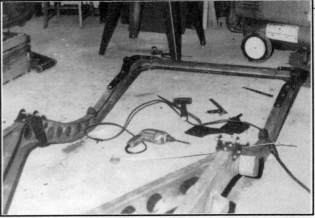

Although the original Ford cross spring will work fine at the rear, the most commonly used modern rearends work better with either semi-elliptic springs or coilover shocks and springs. In this case, semi-elliptics from a Dodge pickup front axle were used at the rear, in combination with a Chassis Engineering mount kit. Short springs, such as the Dodge pickup or 1954-earlier Chevy pickup front are equal length either end, as measured from the centerbolt. Most passenger car springs are longer at the rear than the front, too long for most Fords. Some specialty suppliers, like Posies, have springs made up just for their kits. Plan ahead at this stage, because there are some kits (or your home-made kit) that actually move the pivot points into the frame to bring the rearend lower.

The new crossmember is flat, positioned to become the upper mount for the shock absorbers. Long rear shocks are used because the very best ride/handling is achieved by giving lots of travel to the suspension components. Rule of thumb: Get very soft springing (just enough to support the static car weight), snub travel with heavy duty shocks. In this case, a Chevy Nova rearend is used, which gives a perfect rearend track width when 7-inch wheels are used.

Left-The body was set in place to check wheel/tire clearance at the fenderwell. An extremely wide rear wheel/tire would require wider rear fenders or modifying the frame/fenderwell in pro-street fashion. Another rule of thumb: Always completely rebuild the entire brake system.

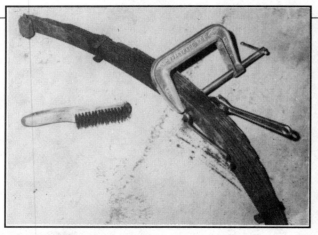

Disassemble a leaf spring; using a C-clamp while the centerbolt is being removed. A new centerbolt will probably be needed, available at nearly any good parts supply.

Use a wire brush and grinder to clean each spring leaf. The lower end of each leaf should be ground round so that it does not dig into the adjacent leaf.

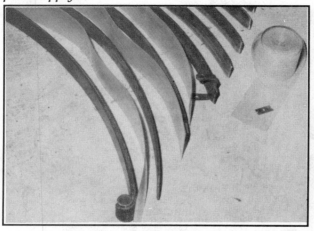

Reassemble the spring with some kind of Teflon insert. Long strips of Teflon can be used, or small Teflon buttons can be used at each leaf tip. Your local spring shop may be able to stamp button depressions in the leaf. Specialty rod suppliers such as Posies have these buttons already in their springs.

Rarely will you find a spring with good shackle bolts. New replacements are available from most parts houses. In this case, a set of Pete and Jake's Polyurethane bushings replace the old Ford swedged rubber type bolts.

Below-Up until 1939, Ford used mechanical brakes. The 1939-'48 Ford hydraulic brakes will interchange on the earlier spindle, as will the much better Lincoln Bendix brakes, and there are a number of rod supplier disc brake kits available.

Below-Since the original 1935 Ford beam axle was being replaced with a Super Bell tube dropped axle, the swap started by cutting off the spring hanger bolt. Invariably, these bolts are stuck in the axle. Grind the torched face of the bolt smooth.

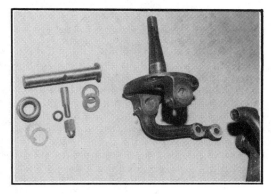

A small drill bit is used to punch a hole dead center of the spring perch bolt. Run this hole into the bolt about 2 inches. Go slow. Increase the drill bit size, and repeat, when the hole is about the size of the perch bolt use a chisel to chip the tapered top part of the bolt out of the axle. At the bottom, the nut will be tapered. Quite often, once a good size hole is drilled in the bolt, it will knock out from the bottom side (or press out). This is usually a tedious, but necessary job. Use a new perch bolt (this really is a misnomer, dating to earlier years when this bolt was really the spring perch), when adding the dropped axle. When the wishbone is cut and widened, the spring hanger (which is ahead of the axle) must be heated and bent outward so the hanger again aligns with the spring. Again, tedious but not difficult.

The key to a really good action on any Ford beam axle suspension is to have new, snug-fitting kingpins. Remember that the bearing goes between the spindle and the bottom side of the axle. Some kits will have bushings that fit the pin just right (a palm push), but sometimes it is necessary to have the bushings honed for final snug fit. When installing the bushings, be sure that the hole in the bushing aligns with the grease zerk hole in the spindle. Too much play at the kingpin usually results in a shimmy of the front wheels.

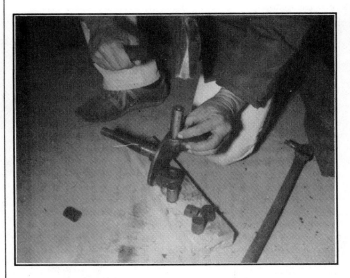

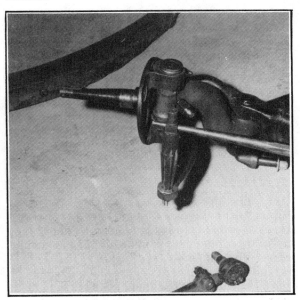

You can do the kingpin replacement at home. Use a piece of bar stock or a correct diameter socket to drive the old bushing out and drift the new bushings in place. Tap gently on the new bushings to keep from rolling the edges. A neat trick is to place the bushings in a freezer for a while before installing.

Once the dropped axle is installed to wishbone and spindle, a trial fit of the tie rods may show tie rod interference at the wishbone. One solution is to use a tie rod end that has a stepped threaded shank, or the steering arm can have the wide part of the taper filled with weld bead, then the arm is re-tapered from the top. This moves the tie rod above the wishbone. But then you must make sure the tie rod does not hit the frame rails or engine oil pan, etc.

Disc brake kits are readily available to mount several different types of discs to the early Ford spindles. Be sure the kit you select is for the spindle you are using (there is a spindle reference elsewhere in this book).

The Ford cross steering is good when it is in perfect condition, but in this case a Saginaw power steering gearbox was substituted. A small adapter plate bolted to the frame does the job. This plate is available from most fat fender Ford suppliers, and it works with either the power or the manual GM gearbox. If the angle of the drag link (from the pitman arm to the right side steering arm) is not correct, bump steer is guaranteed. When the front end swings upward through its operating distance, the tie rod should pass through the mounting point of the steering rod at the pitman arm. The tie rod end can be mounted below or above the pitman arm to get this correct alignment.

All the parts of the front end are temporarily in place, just to check clearances.

For this project, a Buick V6 engine was selected. The driver's side (left) engine mount had to be moved forward for steering box clearance. A piece of plate bolted to the original engine mount holes took care of the problem.

Engine mounts were fabricated from steel plate, arc welded together. Templates of cardboard were made first.

133

Here, the driver's side mount fits to the frame ahead of the Saginaw gearbox.

An odd-fire Buick V6 was used to mock up location of the engine mounts/trans mount. These engines take up about as much space as a small block Chevy V8, but they are an economical alternative for improved gas mileage. Later, a newer Buick even-fire V6 was installed.

Once the engine/trans combination was set in place, the mounts were finished, then the frame and suspension components were disassembled and painted with Imron.

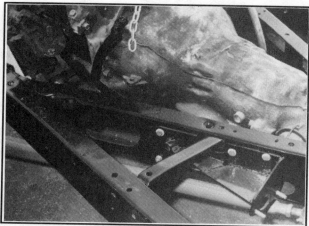

When this car was being built, there was no rod shop brake kit available, so a kit to fit the '33-'34 Ford was modified to fit the '35 frame X-member.

So this is how the chassis looked, with the engine in place. A Chevy disc brake setup is on the Super Bell dropped tube axle up front.

At the rear, the Chevy Nova rearend is supported on semi-elliptic springs, tire sizes are 29-inch diameter rear, 25-inch diameter front.

This is a sedan convertible body, a style that lasted through 1939, but is very rare. Constructed by a coachbuilder, the bodies are composite of available sedan/convertible pieces, so nothing seems to be readily interchangeable. There is lots of wood in these particular open bodies, wood that usually has to be repaired or replaced. That is critical with a four door, in the center doorpost area.

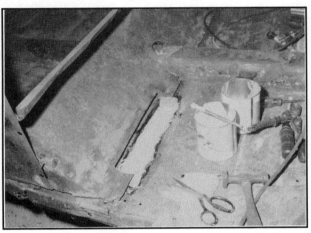

A minor bit of floor cancer was patched in an experiment with the Kwik-Poly system. It works very well, but a metal patch is far better.

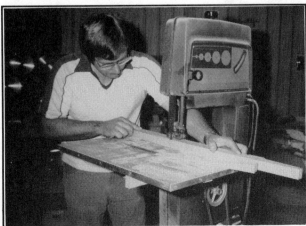

New wood is cut, use only a close grain hardwood for these critical pieces.

The seat is much of the strength of the body, when the wooden/metal framework is removed from the body shell, little remains.

The rotten wood from the center doorpost is removed and used as a pattern.

The replacement doorpost wood is tried for fit. Small adjustments are made with a sander.

Once the new doorpost wood is in place, the metal is cleaned up and the door hinge mounting bolt threads are cleaned with a tap.

The seats of many earlier Fords are a combination of wood and metal. Here, the plywood side pieces and a small lower section of hardwood is bad. The rest of the wood was mostly only discolored and could be re-used.

Inspect all the wood for dry-rot, most of the replacement pieces can be made at home with ordinary tools.

Once the seat assembly is taken apart, any bad wood is immediately apparent. A local cabinet shop will cut pieces, if you don't have the tools. Throw away all the original wood screws, use new screws and glue all joints.

Again, use the original piece of wood as a pattern. If the original is too far gone to use, you'll have to guess-timate.

Here's the replacement seat in place, with all the metal cleaned and painted.

The wood at the rear doorpost and quarter panel area needed complete replacement. An original piece is checked with a tape measure and compared to the opposite side. Sometimes the pieces will not be exactly the same, since these were essentially handbuilt cars.

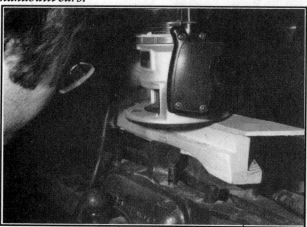

Clamp the wood piece in a vise and use a router to cut out intricate insets.

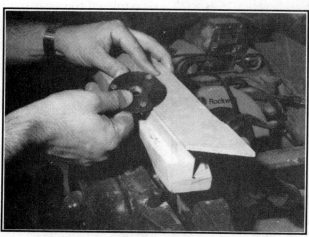

Wood body parts often have metal pieces attached. These pieces should be removed, cleaned and repaired as needed, then attached to the new wood pieces with new wood screws.

For odd shapes of wood, start with hardwood that is thick enough in all directions, draw on the pattern. Much of the original wood pieces will be laminated, a cost-shaving procedure of Ford Motor Co.

This particular curve could have been cut on a band-saw as well as on a router.

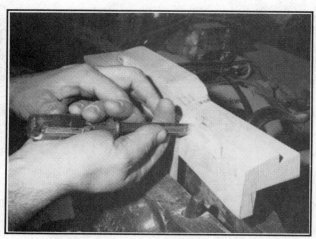

Wood chisels are still needed to make lots of the intricate cuts on special wood framing.

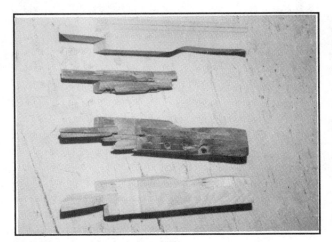

Here, a part of the rear doorpost is shown. On one side, only a small part of the original piece was left. Sometimes, missing areas must be guessed at, a cut-and-try procedure for fitting.

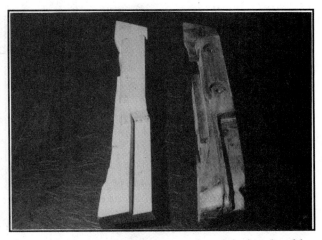

The original piece has been reproduced, holes should be done on a drill press to get accuracy.

The top part of the left rear doorpost is now in place. This wood could be replaced with steel tubing, but that would be a lot of work.

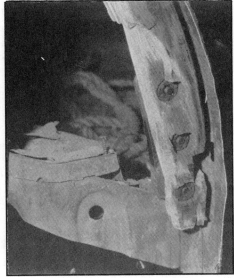

The lower section of rear doorpost is typical of most fat Ford wood, where rot starts in wood most exposed to water.

In this case, the lower piece of wood is tucked away inside the doorpost metal overlay. It should be carefully removed, rebuilt, and replaced.

The package tray area and folding top storage well features wood that is made up of pieces held together by finger joints, glue, and long throughbolts.

Side pieces of the top well are made of flat wood stock that is cut with reliefs to accept the top bows.

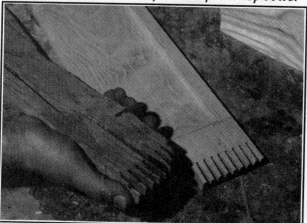

Be careful when making new wood pieces from old wood as a pattern, especially if the original has split. This can and will change measurements.

Once the chassis had been completed, and was rolling, the body was attached. The plan was to make the body fit the frame, so any minor adjustments would need to be in the body structure. With the flooring aligned with frame bolt holes, the door openings were measured and remeasured until all the spaces were constant. Then, the ragged metal around the fender opening was trimmed midpoint of the body roll, so that resulting welding and leading would have minimal warpage.

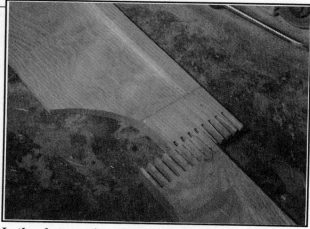

In the absence of a special fingerjoint saw, the joints can be marked off and cut on a bandsaw.

This 1935 Ford sedan convertible body had the rear fender wells removed with a chisel, leaving surrounding metal badly damaged, so much so that restorers would not pay attention to the rest of the body, which was in decent condition. From Wyoming, the body had no rust severe rust.

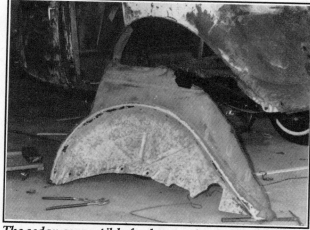

The sedan convertible fender opening is the same as the flatback closed sedan, however the only fender-wells available were from a 1936 sedan. This trunkback sedan is slightly wider at the lower rear corners of the body, but the fender shape is the same.

Although the fenderwells are the same on 1935-'36 Fords, the fenders themselves have a slightly different curve on the crest adjacent to where the taillights mount. Important to a restorer, not so much to a hot rodder. But even these replacement parts, coming from the Rocky Mountains where rust is minor, needed some repair.

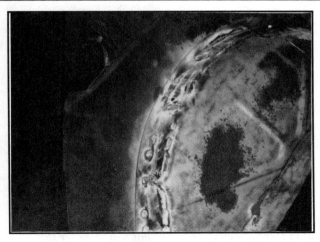

The perimeter of the fenderwells, where the fenders bolt in place, had some rust. Patches were made up and brazed to the perimeter, before the fenderwells were trimmed from surrounding metal.

Next, the surrounding metal was trimmed away adjacent to the body roll at the fenderwell lip. This was done so that actual trimming of the metal at the middle of the body roll would be easier.

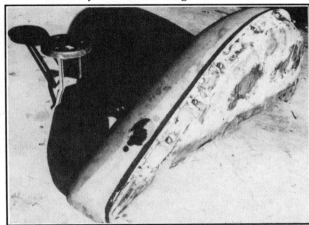

Once the wells were trimmed midpoint of the body roll, the assembly was bolted to the fender. This held the wells in alignment while everything was held to the body for preliminary fitting.

With the fenders still installed on the fenderwells, the wells were tack welded in several places to the body. Where the panels touched the frame, they were bolted in place for additional alignment.

This is a regression photo, to show how plates were welded to the inside of the front portion of each fender well, to get extra strength in areas with rust. These areas are behind wooden doorposts.

The wider 1936 trunkback sedan meant that a portion of the fenderwell at the rear was too wide for the slantback body. At this point, the fenders bolt to the flat inner surface of the well, so a long pie shape cut was made in the fenderwell and it was narrowed to fit the body. No effect on the fender fit.

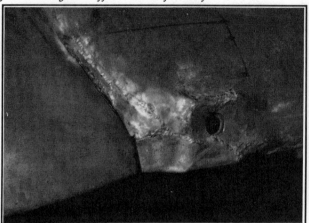

After the fenderwells were in place, additional metal was welded to the torn body panels and some rough shaping done with a hammer.

Here, the fenderwell insert has been finish welded completely. The rear doorpost area was checked time and again during fenderwell installation, to make sure it was not moving due to heat. Braces of thin wall tubing could have been used if some absolute reference points had been available.

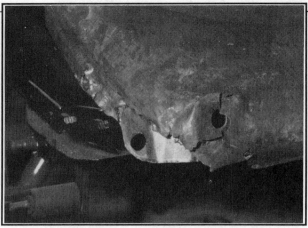

With the original fenderwells gone, the body had taken severe damage at the rear corners. As the fenderwells were being fit, inner support metal was created for the body corners.

With all the rough shaping done, the body began to look pretty good again. It is amazing what patience will do when trying to save a fat Ford body.

Once the fenderwells are finish welded, the surfaces are cleaned with a body grinder. Low and high spots are hammered smooth so that only a thin coating of lead will be required. Lead is used because this is an area that can take a beating, and plastic filler will not stand up to such use.

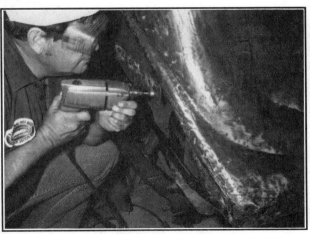

For leading, it it imperative that every tiny area of metal be perfectly clean, here small sanding tips are used in a drill motor.

Then, rotary files are used to get down in tiny pockmarks. Absolutely every part of the surface must be cleaned prior to tinning the surface. If there is an area that is not tinned properly, the lead will not stick.

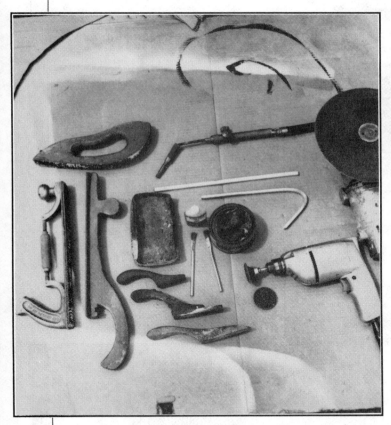

These are the tools used in leading. The reason for using lead is that on corners and places where damage could occur, the lead is as strong as the base metal, whereas plastic filler will easily crack and chip away. Use the lead in such places, then very thin coats of plastic filler elsewhere to get a perfectly smooth surface. When working lead, use the vixen files until you become proficient. Although lead is getting hard to locate, except through specialty mail-order houses, some older body shops and shop suppliers often have some tucked away in a corner.

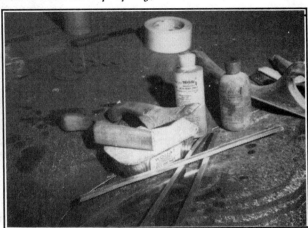

Most lead available today comes in small rectangular bars, and it is quite expensive. A star-shape cross-section to the bar is preferred, as it melts easier.

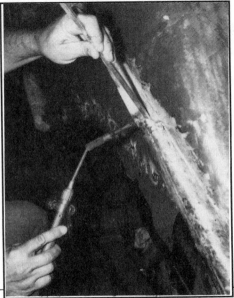

Use a soft flame, heat the metal slightly, then concentrate the flame in an alternating fashion between metal and lead bar. Sort of gob the melted lead onto the surface.

Then heat the lead gob until it softens (this takes practice and is the real key to leading) and paddle the lead into shape. Keep the paddle surface covered with beeswax so it doesn't stick to the lead.

A curved lead file is used to make the round surface smooth. Go slow and check the work often.

Below-When a body is damaged badly, it is wise to make up templates of cardboard so that one side can be made the same as the other side. Here, lines were made on the body, the same place each side, then the cardboard templates were trimmed and marked for each station.

A long flat file is used on the edge of the body roll, pull the file toward you to get the shaping just right until you become an expert.

144

Tex Smith's HOT ROD LIBRARY

Shipped UPS for quick delivery, add $3 postage for each book ordered

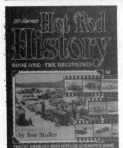

Hot Rod History

The legends of hot rodding are raving about this new book! Although the very first hot rod was created when the first automobile was built, it is generally agreed that the modern hot rod sport got its big push during the late 1920s and 1930s. But until recently, any kind of history of hot rodding was ignored. Not now. With over 200 pages literally crammed cover-to-cover, Tex Smith's Hot Rod History traces the hobby from Ed Winfield in the Twenties through activity in the early Fifties. First of an on-going series, this volume by Tom Medley will become the most read book in any rodder's library. Featuring such legends as Kong Jackson, Spalding Brothers, Wes Cooper, Bruce Johnston, Bob Stelling, Alex Xydias, Ray Brown, Wally Parks, etc, etc. Photos and facts to delight the most astute historian, but most of all, this is a book that is just plain fun to read

Hot RodHistory Softbound.................$17.95
Limited edition hardbound...................$26.95, $3.50 shipping
(Allow 8-12 weeks delivery.)

Automotive Art

Every male, from 13 to 85, loves to draw cars. But there hasn't been a real book on automotive art for nearly 40 years. How To Draw Cars cures the problem. Over 200 pages of magic, showing everything anyone needs to know to go from simple doodle to professional drawing. This is the book that dreams are made of, and it is the perfect gift, even for the non-artist. Covers everything from hot rods to dream cars to sports cars and racers. Another absolute must-have for the complete car library.

How To draw Cars.............$17.95

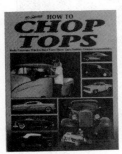

Chopping Tops

This is the only book on the subject available, and it is a runaway best seller. Over 200 pages, with step-by-step guidelines for hammering the lid on rods and customs, as well as pickups. Tops fit into 3 basic categories, so what applies to one marque applies to most other makes with the same style top. Covers cars from the Twenties/Thirties through today. How To Chop Tops has become the instant "bible" of rodders and customizers around the world.

How To Chop Tops..........$17.95

For Mopar Nuts

If you're into Chrysler Corporation hot rods and customs, then How To Build Chrysler/Plymouth/Dodge Hot Rods is for you. There is no other book like this one, with a concentration on nothing but Mopar products. It is the first of a series, and guaranteed to give you more information than any other source. Packed with how-to's and photos.

How To Build Chrysler/Plymouth/Dodge Hot Rods..........$17.95

Basic Customizing

The number 1 book in a special series for car enthusiasts, How To Build Custom Cars has quickly become the modern "bible" for the hobby, appealing to the home builder and professional alike. Covers everything from chassis swaps and frame clips to fender flares and sectioning, grille swaps, upholstery...over 200 pages jam packed with nothing but custom car building information. The only total custom book on the market.

How To Build Custom Cars..................$17.95

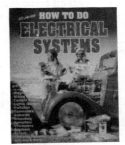

Wiring Rods/Customs/Kit Cars

Automotive electrics can be a huge problem, even for the experts. How To Do Electrical Systems takes the mystery out of the process with easy to read diagrams. Anyone can use the book to wire and troubleshoot practically any special built car. Wiring schematics for myriad accessories common to the contemporary rod or custom. The troubleshooting section makes this an invaluable "on board" companion for every builder.

How To Do Electical Systems................$13.00

Basic Hot Rodding

How To Build Real Hot Rods is the number 1 book in this series, with an emphasis on low cost how-to's aimed at the home builder. Crammed with information that beginners need and advanced rodders use as reference. Everything is included, from frames to suspension to bodywork and upholstery. This is a "must have" book for any rod enthusiast's library, the foundation for more advanced building.

How To Build Real Hot Rods.........$15.00

For Chevy Folks

Like all our books, How To Build CHEVY HOT RODS is for the person who is really into the subject. We cover the full span of Chevy street rod potentials, from the Twenties to the Fifties. From basics of rewooding the early bodies to suspension components for the shoeboxes. Everthing is covered, to get the Chevy enthusiast on the way to highway fun. Nothing is in this book but information about Chevrolet hot rods. Packed with how-to's and photos.

How To Build Chevy Hot Rods...$17.95

Just around the Corner

Coming right away is our in-depth book on How To Build FAT FORDS 1935-48, How To Build SHOEBOX FORDS AND MERCS 1949-54, the new CAMARO SUPPLEMENT, a book on SPORTS SPECIALS, and a host of new titles for 1991.

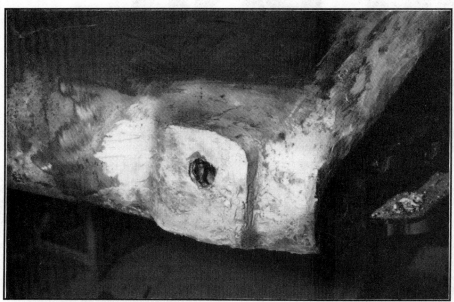

Lead build-up over damaged metal can be checked with the templates. Then as the lead is filed away, the templates are used to make sure the finished shape is the same on both sides.

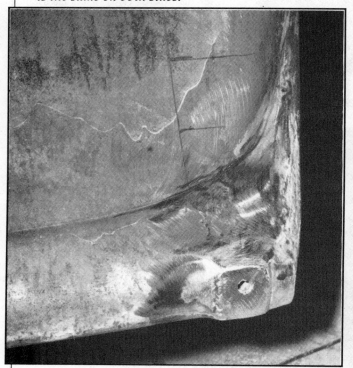

Left-As with plastic filler, do not use too much lead. Instead, work the metal into shape as much as possible.

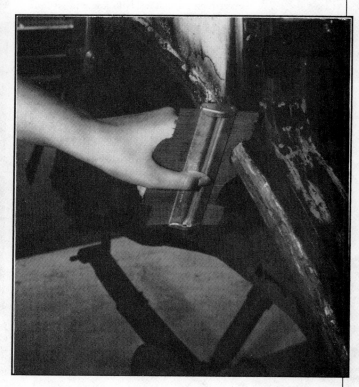

Right-An adjustable template is used to check the body roll as it is shaped.

Now it is time to start doing the finish metalwork on the body. These are the tools most commonly used, most of them are old pieces scrounged from retiring bodymen. New hammers and dollies are not too expensive, however.

After all that work, the fenderwell is in place. In total time, doing both wells took about two days.

Above-This is how the project looks as the rear panel is ready for finish body work. All of the old paint will be removed during the course of getting the shape back.

Good body and fender straightening starts with feel, the feel of the metal as the hand is moved over the surface. Use a dolly behind the panel and a body hammer on the face (do not use any other kind of hammer!), raise or lower deformed spots by lightly working the area. Go slow, be patient.

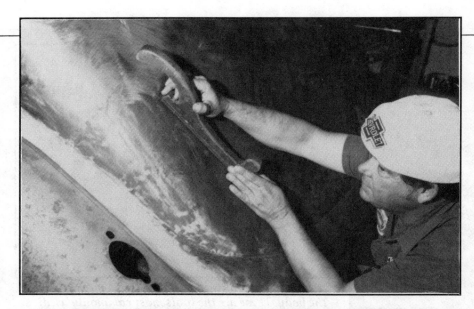

Until you are good with a body grinder, use a vixen file across the metal surface. It will show high and low spots immediately.

When using a body grinder, tilt the head slightly, use only light pressure, do not stay in one spot long enough to get the metal hot, or you will create warpage that is hard to remove.

Work a spot, feel it with the hand, then work it some more. Once you get some experience with this procedure, it is quite rapid.

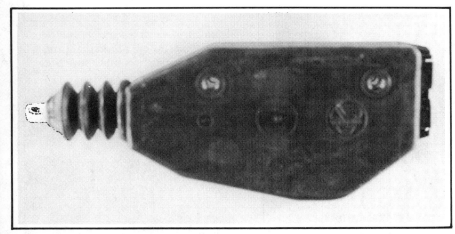

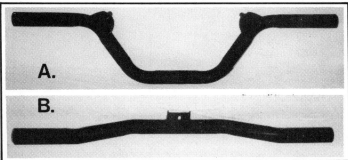

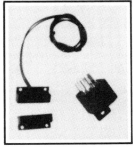

Finally, use thin coats of plastic filler to get the entire surface perfect. When the filler is sanded away, there should be only the slightest hint of a filler.

As the project takes shape, small areas of metal are worked. Again, always measure to make sure that everything fits.

Old Ford gas tanks definitely should be given a cleaning. Quite often it will be found that the lower part of the tank has rusted away from the inside and is paper thin.

The doors, fenders and some small items were taken to a chemical stripper. Although the doors did not have rust, the panels were not in perfect shape. At first, it was thought that regular four door sedan panels could be used for new skins, but inspection showed that the sedan convert used different size doors than the closed cars.

Extra engine clearance was needed at the firewall. The original depression was correct depth but needed more sideways clearance.

A carbide blade fitted to a Skil saw was used to make the firewall metal cuts. Firewalls are of heavy gauge material.

Left- Here, the original firewall recess curved edges have been moved outward to the corners and tack welded in place.

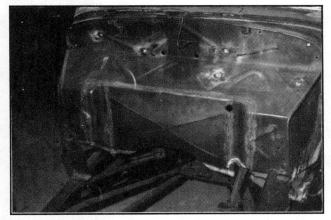

Above-A section of flat 16-gauge metal was cut to size, then an Eastwood bead roller put an X-shape in the panel to eliminate oil-canning. Then everything was finish welded.

Holes in the cowl panel area were left over from an antenna. These were filled with metal patches, then smoothed and covered with thin coat of plastic filler.

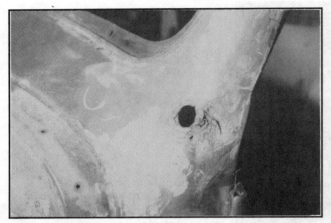

Windshield post had a hole from a spotlight. This is in an area that was full of original factory lead.

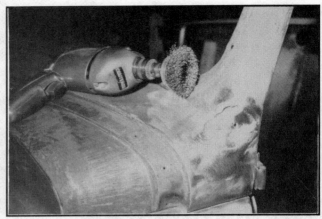

The lead was melted away, then the hole filled with a metal patch. On specialty bodies, you will find a great deal of lead used for shaping. The windshield posts on this sedan convert were thick with lead.

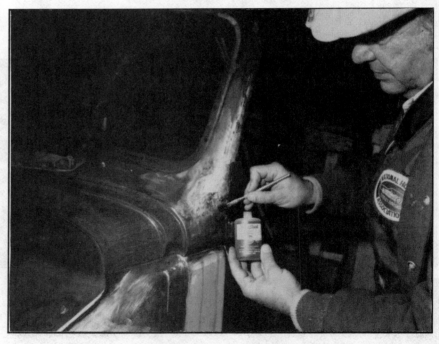

The metal patch was tinned with acid, then lead was added to return post to original shape.

Bottom left-Cowl panel and kickpanel area were worked with hammer and dolly, then smoothed with plastic filler.

Bottom right-With the body in good condition, attention was returned to the chassis. It was decided to fit the frame with a Mustang front suspension, using a Gene Reese kit (now out of business). There are a lot of kits available for IFS in fat Fords.

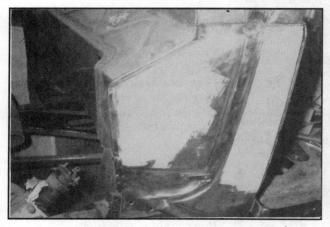

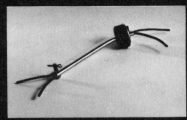

153

A transmission cooler was set into the frame under the passenger side flooring.

Fuel line and brake line tuck inside the frame rails. Keep these away from heat, and use clamps liberally.

Kits for mounting fat Ford bodies are available from restoration and rod suppliers. This kit includes cork gasket along the side rails and rubber gaskets on the X-member.

A Midland brake booster was used, along with a Kelsey-Hayes brake proportioning valve, since this car used drum rear/disc front brakes. It is not essential to use a power booster, if a correct size master cylinder and appropriate brake pedal ratio are employed.

Take extra time with all the plumbing and minor details of the chassis, because it is much easier to do the work with the body out of the way.

At the front, a power rack and pinion Mustang steering is used. Although not essential on this particular car, it is advisable on the larger, heavier fat Fords.

As with many projects of this nature, about the time this car was seeing light in the tunnel, it was sold. John Rutledge of the Kernville, California area bought the project and set it aside while other cars were being built. Then, several years later, work started again, with some changes John wanted. The rear spring hangers were moved higher on the frame (to lower the car in back), late model seats were substituted, etc. At the time of this article, the car was progressing nicely. It will probably be seen at western rod runs throughout the 1990s decade.

157

CLASS OF '50

Vehicle: 1936 Ford 3-Window
Owner: Rholand Lange — Brigham City, Utah

This 1936 Ford is so named because that's when Rholand graduated from High school, and his best buddy had one just like it, and they double dated in the car, and.... 'Nuff said.

More than a dozen years ago, Rholand bought this coupe for $250, and the results you see here are all his labor, except for the paint (Dennis Heirschie of Perry, Utah) and the upholstery (Donny VanCamp, Ogden, Utah).

Rholand started by totally disassembling the car, then replacing bad frame parts. A complete '64 Fairlane 8-inch rearend with springs was added, along with air shocks (one reason this baby scrapes the pavement when desired!). Up front, a stock '36 axle was upfitted with disc brakes. Six leaves were removed from the front springs, then Teflon was added between spring leaves. This dropped the front 2-1/2 inches.

Strips of 1/16-inch Teflon were put between the remaining spring leaves, to ensure a smooth ride. A Vega steering with cross link was adapted to the frame, and brackets were made for the '69 Ford Windsor 351-inch V8 and '64 Ford C4 automatic transmission (with '66 Mustang shifter).

The engine got a Crower cam and lifters/springs under an Offenhauser 360 manifold, with 600 cfm Holley carb. The air cleaner and polished valve covers are Cobra, while ignition is dual-point Mallory. Rholand put in 150 hours of head work, getting the intake and exhaust ports polished, and a progressive angle valve job. The driveshaft is out of a '64 Ford Fairlane.

With the chassis rolling on P195-75R15 front and 195-50R15 rear tires, attention was turned to the body. The firewall was cut back flush for more engine room, and stainless steel waffle plate was cut to fit. The front fender inner panels, upper and lower grille inserts, X-member covers, and air cleaner bonnet are also stainless, as are the dash face, throttle pedal, and license plate backing.

A new floorpan was needed. The trunk lid was converted to a rumble seat (remember that buddy's car), the spare tire mount was removed, and

The body was only subtly modified, and from this angle it's hard to notice the differences from a stock '36. Black Imron was treated to a faint blue flame job that is nearly invisible.

The trunk of this classy '36 was converted to a rumble seat, reminiscent of an old friend's car from high school days. Stock running board rubber was removed, and holes filled to give a smooth appearance.

short bumper brackets fashioned. Stock running board rubber was removed and all the holes filled, for a smooth finish. Fender skirts were handmade.

With all the body work completed, everything got a covering of Black Imron. Later, the faintest of blue flames were added for a very, very subtle touch.

The interior is a light grey velour and Naugahyde over Chevy swivel seats. Cadillac Eldorado wood trim with pull handles are found on the doors, along with Buick red/white door lights and Lincoln courtesy lights. The window frames are chromed, and the radio speakers are behind the upholstery. Incidentally, the stock Ford type radio head with cables operates an AM/FM cassette radio hidden behind the dash.

Wherever this car goes, it creates a crowd of pleased spectators. Probably people who remember a buddy's car they once dated in.

A '69 Ford 351 Windsor V8 was stuffed under the hood, and outfitted with a Mallory dual-point ignition, Crower cam, Offenhauser 360 manifold and Holley 600 cfm carburetor. Cobra valve covers look great in this engine cage.

Doors are trimmed with Cadillac Eldorado wood and pull handles. Light grey velour and Naugahyde upholstery covers everything, including Chevy swivel seats.

Machine-turned stainless steel dash face sets some sparkle to the interior. Behind the stock radio head is an AM/FM cassette stereo system that is controlled by the stock knobs.

Handmade fender skirts completely hide the tires, as this '36 gets down in the weeds. Air shocks help control ride height, so Rholand can put it on the ground if he wants to.

FLAMING LADY

by Jim Ingalls

Vehicle: 1936 Ford 3-Window Coupe
Owner: Jim Ingalls — Twin Falls, Idaho

Subtle flames are visible on the doors of Flaming Lady, pictured here at Shoshone Falls, Idaho. Two-inch top chop gets the profile down, yet allows plenty of visibility from the driver's seat.

I think my obsession with chopped '36 Ford 3-window coupes started in 1948, when I was 4 years old riding a tricycle on the sidewalks of Inglewood, California. There were two tan coupes in town (one was a dry lakes record holder), and that apparently imprinted on my mind and has haunted me ever since.

Through the years, I've had a number of rods, but no '36s. Finally, I bought a '36 coupe in Denver. Since our cars don't rust in Idaho, I didn't check this Colorado car very carefully. After 5 years of wasted motion, the car went down the road to a braver person than myself.

In May of 1986, things fell into place. This car came from the collection of an elderly gentleman who had half a dozen '36s and agreed to sell it because it was missing too many original parts. Perfect for a street rod, and it was rust free. As if the previous false start hadn't been enough, I built the '36 chassis with a Mustang II independent front suspension (consuming 6 months of time) and then changed my mind. Here I had the car I'd always wanted, and I couldn't decide on the running gear! Seems my clear ideal was being muddied by reading too many street rod magazines. The final decision was to build an old-time rod, basic and simple, with a few modern conveniences thrown in.

The chassis features a Vintage Chassis Works 4-inch dropped axle with Volare rotors and Chevelle calipers. This is one of the few combinations that is narrow enough to clear the fat fenders of a low '36. Chassis Engineering provided the split wishbone kit, reverse eye spring, semi-elliptic rear springs, and front and rear sway bars. A Vega steering box and Pete and Jakes shock kit finish the front. Out back, a '66 Mustang rearend with 3.25:1 gears has been fitted with a Street Rod Mfg. Co. disc parking brake. Surprisingly, these rearends are a little too narrow for fat fender Fords, unless you run reversed rims. I ended up with 3-inch lowering blocks, to get the right stance.

Exhaust is 2-inch pipe from a set of TCI tuck-in headers. The turbo mufflers were a little ratty, so we turned them backward — no noticeable change in performance, and much quieter. Wheels are solids 5x15 and 8x15, with big and little radials. Although the car sits low, it handles great even without independent front or rear suspension.

Traditional go-power comes from a '59 Chevy small block, bored to 301 cubic inches, running a Duntov cam and three 2-barrel carburetors. More modern is the beefed-up TH350 automatic transmission. If you try this combination, be warned that the early block must be drilled and tapped to accept a starter. One of the few things done right the first time on this project was to run a 3/8-inch fuel line for the multiple carbs. I've had good luck with cheap radiators, so I had the stocker cleaned, checked, and a 7-pound pressure cap installed.

Trying to decide how much to chop the 3-window top was tough. A compromise to retain ample visibility was a 2-inch cut, with a nearly flat Toronado top filling the center section, to give an overall lower profile. The original car needed to have a new firewall, so I installed one from Bitchin' Products, and it worked out perfectly. The final body mods were a leaded spare tire mount and deck handle, louvered hood, and sunken electric antenna.

When it came time to paint the car of my dreams, guess what? I couldn't decide on color! My teenage daughters voted for the two-tone, which is Centauri enamel Black and '87 Mazda Sunrise Red.

I had a lot of old timey parts, including a set of '37 DeSoto bumpers, only to find that they are too wide and it takes two fronts. Suddenly, I liked stockers best. The bull nose is an old $9.95 J.C. Whitney piece. To finish off the exterior, I installed '47 Ford hubcaps and beauty rings from Bob Drake. Pinstripe flames were done by local artist Jeff Devey, and a ton of credit is due an old buddy, Bill Patterson, for the chop and paint.

The interior was done in Empress velour by Dr. Joe, another Idaho talent. The seat is a Rod Tin reproduction, while the rumble seat is original. I made an aluminum panel for the VDO Cockpit gauges, and air conditioning/heat are provided by a Vintage Air unit. Other luxuries include a Porsche stereo system, Zemco cruise control, and '64 Buick Riviera tilt wheel.

The girls thought the car reminded them of the poem about the lady bug with its house on fire, so they named it Flaming Lady.

Exhaust is 2" pipe from a set of TCI tuck-in headers, and turbo mufflers turned backward to improve noise control without any ill effect on performance.

Flaming Lady definitely has a seating limitation, but that just goes with the territory when you own a 3-window coupe. Seat is a Rod Tin reproduction, covered in Empress velour.

Small block engine is from a '59 Chevy, bored to 301 cubes and decked out with a trio of 2-barrel carburetors. Inside is a Duntov cam.

Jim built an aluminum panel to contain a selection of VDO Cockpit gauges. Air and heat are by Vintage Air. Other luxuries include a Porsche stereo system, Zemco cruise control, and '64 Riviera tilt wheel.

'37 CLUB COUPE

Vehicle: 1937 Ford Club Coupe
Owner: Joe Vinson — Boise, Idaho

Since a motorcycle accident broke Joe's back, he has had to perform his work from a wheelchair. But that didn't stop him when it came to fulfilling his desire to build his own street rod.

In 1965, a motorcycle accident, resulting in a broken back, took away Joe Vinson's ability to use his legs. But it couldn't take away his enthusiasm for cars and the desire to build a street rod of his own. Evidence of his accomplishment can be seen on these pages.

Even under the best conditions, building a car is a difficult task. Imagine not being able to stand up while working! That takes a lot more dedication to the project than most folks can muster. Also, building a single street rod during a lifetime is quite an accomplishment, but this is Joe's second time around since the accident.

Joe is owner of Autobody Specialists in Boise, Idaho, where he has been involved in the management of the collision repair business since 1972. Being in an automotive business such as this is an advantage because it helps expand a person's understanding of what makes a car work. For Joe, it also put him in direct contact with people who could help with aspects of the project that he couldn't do by himself.

During the formative stages, Joe dismantled the entire car, laid each piece on the table and went to work on it. He personally did all the finish work on the car, with the exception of the roof. One of his bodymen, Rick Loven, chopped the top. Nephew, Ed Murphy, painted the car (with the help of some expert guidance), using yellow Centauri acrylic urethane basecoat and Du-Pont Euroclear topcoat.

The drivetrain consists of a 327 Chevy engine, TH350 automatic transmission with a shift kit, and a Ford 9-inch rearend. The front axle is a 4-inch dropped I-beam, and Toyota Celica power steering and power brake units were employed.

On the inside, a Speedway Motors instrument panel was set into the stock dash. Joe built the hand-control system to replace foot functions when driving the car, and the driver's bucket seat was rigged to swivel on an old Chevy Citation spindle to allow him to fit his wheelchair behind the seat.

All this only goes to prove that you can't keep a good hot rodder down.

Below-Joe fabricated hand controls to allow him take care of all the functions normally taken care of by foot. The driver's side bucket seat pivots on a Chevy Citation spindle to allow him to fit his wheelchair behind the seat.

Original factory price for a 1937 Ford club coupe was only $720. We'd dare say that Joe Vinson's example of this car is worth considerably more.

Below-A Chevy 327 V8 engine under the hood is backed up by a TH350 automatic transmission that has been kitted for better shifting. Torque then proceeds rearward to a Ford 9-inch rearend.

A moderate top chop lowered the lid enough to squeeze the glass down to narrow vision slits. With bumpers removed, the '37 takes on a slick, aerodynamic appearance.

Right-Hood sides were cleaned up of their stock vents, and louvers were punched in the top of the hood to release engine compartment heat. Shortie wipers keep the V-butted windshield clear.

RARE RED ROD

by James Handy

Vehicle: 1937 Ford Club Coupe
Owner: Lee Bettencourt — Fresno, California

It is the exception when a rare early model from one of the Detroit Biggies is transformed into a street rod showpiece, instead of getting the full restoration treatment. During the 1937 model year, Ford produced only about 16,000 Club Coupes like the one on these pages. The Club Coupe is extremely well proportioned and pleasing to the eye from almost any angle.

The detailed stock chassis has been painted black, and features a Super Bell axle up front and a Mustang rearend. Late Chevy disc brakes flank each end of the 4-inch dropped Super Bell, while Mustang steering controls direction. The steering column was donated by a 1972 Chevrolet. Motive power comes from a 327 cubic inch small block, hooked up to a TH350 automatic transmission.

The unusual Club Coupe body was ironed out and sprayed with red acrylic lacquer by the owner, in his first attempt at painting a car. The stock headlights now sport quartz bulbs, for improved night driving visibility. Interior and dash are close to stock, except for the owner-fabricated rear seat riser, steering column mount, and stereo console. Upholstery is saddle brown velour and Naugahyde, with stitch work performed by Rocky's Interiors in Fresno, California. The car was pinstriped in gold leaf, which nicely accents the bright red lacquer. Making the ground connection are 5x15 and 7x15 McLean chromed wire wheels, wrapped in Winston steel radials.

Just goes to show you what a body can do if he puts his mind to it. Lee Bettencourt wanted an unusual street rod, using an uncommon Ford body style. We think he has built one classy ride, and it kind of makes us want to go out looking for a fat fendered Ford coupe to work on.

Interior was stitched together in tan Naugahyde and saddle brown velour. Features include door pockets, center and overhead consoles, Audi seats, and Marantz stereo system.

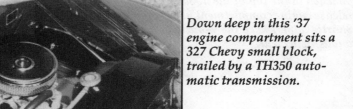

Down deep in this '37 engine compartment sits a 327 Chevy small block, trailed by a TH350 automatic transmission.

Teardrop headlights and one-piece grille are definitely 1937 Ford, but the headlights have been treated to halogen bulbs for improved night driving visibility. Four-inch dropped Super Bell axle gets the front end down in the weeds.

Tracking down grille parts, headlights and hood ornaments is no easy task on the more rare "late model" Fords, but this one is complete in the exterior trim department.

The bright red California jewel looks good from any angle. McLean wire wheels are a nice touch that add sparkle and an old timey flavor to the car.

Very little was done to modify the exterior of the '37 Club Coupe, but a peek inside and under the hood immediately separates this rod from the restored car category.

MIXING BUSINESS & PLEASURE

Vehicle: 1937 Ford Business Coupe
Owner: Jack Ketlinski — Boise, Idaho

Dressed to impress in Centerline wheels, a bright coat of red and grab-ya graphics, this '37 Ford business coupe is a clear demonstration of what can be done with a vehicle type that has not always enjoyed the highest regard in the street rod world.

Once upon a time, a business coupe was the last thing a budding street rodder wanted sitting in his driveway. Looking back, it's hard to say why that was so, but it's like so many other near-sighted attitude problems that can develop in a hobby like ours. Fortunately, there are guys like Jack Ketlinski whose attitude eyesight is 20/20. One look at Jack's fine example of a '37 Ford business coupe, and it's tough to imagine why anybody would pass up one of these beauties.

Jack has a street rod shop in Boise, Idaho where several cars have been built. Each has been a project for the entire family. Most of the mechanical work done on this particular car was performed by son Tim.

After being rescued from a life of obscurity, the car was stripped from its frame for a proper application of rod building. As it stands today, this '37 is essentially a brand new car, having been completely rebuilt from the ground up.

Power comes from a balanced high-performance 225-cid Buick V6 that has been hopped up with a Smoky Yunick/Weiand intake, Crane cam, and TRW pistons. Headers are by Suchy, and the exhaust system is stainless steel. All braided hoses and lines come from Earls, and the stainless steel fuel tank was made by Johnny Van Etten.

The interior is done in grey leather and Mercedes mohair, with upholstery work by Alan Lueck of Comfort Specialists. Air Teaque provided the air conditioner for those hot southern Idaho summer days. A late Chevrolet steering column offers the convenience of tilt wheel adjustment. Power brakes (discs in front) are from Midland Power.

Going down the road, this is one fine looking rod. Centerline Champ 500 wheels are an eye-catching attraction. But the bright red paint job by Mike Nyborg, graphics by Paul Stoll, and pinstriping by Jeff Dewey turn heads in a big way.

There is no doubt about it, Jack Ketlinski knows how to mix business with pleasure.

Trick stuff includes front power disc brakes from Midland Power. A peek beneath the floor would reveal a stainless steel exhaust system and stainless steel fuel tank.

This car is essentially brand new, having been stripped all the way down and rebuilt piece by piece. Body side graphics are by Paul Stoll, with pinstriping by Jeff Dewey.

Under the hood is a balanced high-performance Buick V6. Intake is by Smokey Yunick and Weiand. Braided hoses and lines are from Earls.

HAMMRRD '38

by Rich Johnson

Vehicle: 1938 Ford 2-Door Sedan
Owner: Mike Lynch — Northlake, Illinois

What started out as a relatively stock street rod, bearing a vanity plate that read Fat A Tak, went under the hacksaw and now wears a plate that reads Hammrrd. But the vanity plate isn't all that was changed. In fact, before and after photos leave one wondering if this is actually the same car. What a dramatic transformation!

When Mike Lynch bought the car for $5500, it was solid but hid a few surprises. Nevertheless, Mike had a mental vision of what it could look like with a little work. As it turned out, a little work became 4 years worth of labor, but it was all worth it. With the constant help of his wife (who donated her nails to the project), Mike ended up with a dynamite ride that attracts attention wherever it goes. Throughout the entire building process, the car remained driveable, except for intermittent times when it was torn down for major work.

During the first year of building, Mike concentrated his efforts on mechanical upgrades. Chassis work included installation of a Mustang II front end, which brought with it the advantages of disc brakes and rack and pinion steering. The rear axle had been a Chevy unit, which was swapped out and a Ford 8-inch installed. A Posie kit upgraded the rear suspension. American Outlaw wheels were fit with Sun Specs knock offs, and the combination is dazzling.

Under previous ownership, the '38 street rod had received a heart transplant in the form of a Chevy 283 V8 engine and Powerglide transmission. Mike decided to beef up the power department by installing a Chevy 350 V8 and TH350 automatic tranny.

The second year, Mike worked out all the details of the top chop and body modifications, which he performed himself. Mike dropped the top 5 inches, retaining the rain gutters but removing all the rest of the car's trim. Door handles were removed, and remote power windows installed to gain entry. The cowl was filled, as was the crank hole, the grille was made into a one-piece unit, and a recessed rear license plate chamber fabricated. The hood nose was extended 5 inches, homemade boxes were built for the taillights, with lens material cover-

In 1986, Mike bought this previously owned street rod for $5500 as a solid base to use for building Hammrrd. Then, he spent the next four years making it what we see here.

168

ing slots cut in the body, and a frenched third brake light installed. The windshield was V-butted and installed in the original frame, and a '46 Ford fuel door found a home on the left rear fender. Smooth running boards round out the clean appearance of the car, and when it came time for paint, the running boards were treated to the flame theme.

It was during the third year of construction that the paint work was accomplished. Mike painted the car at home, with the help of friend Dennis Lass. Colors are described by Mike as Yuk Yellow with Magenta flames (actually Panther Pink), and pinstriping by Tom Kelly.

Whatever the colors are called, the effect is striking.

It wasn't until the fourth year that the interior was completed. Ron Grubb did the upholstery work, and a Springfield dash panel was filled with VDO gauges. An IDIDIT tilt/telescoping column was installed for driver comfort. Vintage Air provided the heat and air conditioning system.

With the project complete, the '38 called Hammrrd has taken on a whole new appearance. It's now long, low and snakey looking. It sports the benefits of late technology, great graphics, and a superb fat profile. And that's what it's all about.

After a year had been spent concentrating on mechanical upgrades, Mike tore into the top chop project. The lid was lowered five inches, and a number of other body mods performed.

Look how much impact a five inch top chop can have. Amazingly, throughout the project, the car was kept in driveable condition most of the time, except when it was torn down for major work, such as in this photo.

Chassis upgrades include the installation of a Mustang II front end, compete with disc brakes and rack and pinion steering. A Ford 8-inch rearend was used out back, with a Posie kit for suspension improvement.

Replacing the earlier 283 Chevy V8 and Poweglide combination is this 350 cid V8 Chevy engine, followed by a TH350 automatic transmission. There's just enough chrome to add sparkle under the hood.

Homebuilt boxes were fitted behind the rear panel to house the taillights. Lens material is fitted into slots cut in the body. Note the flush-fitting third brake light above the deck lid. A recessed license plate housing is filled with the new vanity plate.

Chopped top and narrow slot windows filled with tinted glass give Hammrrd a snakey appearance. Smooth running boards carry the flame paint theme that graces the rest of the car's nose.

'39 HAWK

by John Lee

Vehicle: 1939 Ford Coupe
Owner: Dan Hix — Pittsburg, Kansas

Don't let the Dove Gray lacquer job mislead you, this '39 coupe is really a hawk under the skin. Dan Hix builds his cars to perform, and this one does it with a .060" overbored 327 Chevy with Jahns 11:1 pistons on balanced and polished rods. The Crane cam, lifters and springs work stock valves in cc'd heads. A Camaro Z-28 manifold provides a mount for the Holley 600 carb. J.T. Winfrey modified the TH350 transmission and also installed wiring and a Vintage Air cooling system.

This potent combination is mounted in a chassis that was constructed by Alan Grove and Curt Cunningham. A 3-inch dropped Super Bell axle with Chevelle disc brakes attaches to the stock '39 frame via split wishbone and Gabriel shocks. A narrowed 9-inch Ford rearend was fitted with Summers Brothers axles, then mounted with Gabriels and parallel leaf springs. BFGoodrich radials on American Spirit 8x15 rear and 6x14 front wheels remain neatly inside the fenders on all four corners.

A big boost to the new wave of popularity '39-'40 model Fords are enjoying is the availability of over the counter parts. Dan employed several in his '39, including fiberglass fenders by Wescott and a machined aluminum instrument panel, valve covers, pulleys, air cleaner and wheel knock-offs by The Carriage Works.

Left stock, except for the swap to '40 headlights, the body was restored by Dan Kennedy and Peter Wietz, then painted by Kennedy. The contrasting interior in maroon vinyl was rolled and pleated in the original style by Bob Sipes. A Chevy van gave up its steering column and wheel to the project, and VDO gauges complete the interior appointments.

Having built a number of early Ford rods, including '29 and '32 roadsters and a '32 coupe, Dan is now in the fat fender beauty parade with this slick '39.

Mostly stock in the body, except for a swap to Wescott fiberglass fenders and a set of '40 Ford headlights, this '39 coupe was restored by Dan Kennedy and Peter Wietz, then painted Dove Gray by Kennedy.

Below-Chassis was constructed by Alan Grove and Curt Cunningham. A 3-inch drop Super Bell axle was treated to a set of Chevelle disc brakes. Rear axle is a narrowed Ford 9-inch. Wheels are American Spirit, wrapped with BFGoodrich radial rubber.

Contrasting interior was done in maroon vinyl, using the stock seat as a foundation. Bob Sipes did the stitch work in a traditional roll and pleat style.

Steering column and wheel came out of a Chevy van. VDO gauges fill a special one-off machined aluminum dashboard that was built by The Carriage Works.

Under the hood is a .060" overbored Chevy 327, stuffed with Jahns 11:1 pistons on balanced and polished rods. Crane cam, lifters and springs push stock valves in cc'd heads. Dress-up is thanks to aluminum valve covers, pulleys and air cleaner, all by The Carriage Works.

GLASS FROM THE PAST

by John Lee

Vehicle: 1939 Ford Convertible Replica
Owner: Dwight Bond — Gibbon, Nebraska

Since founding Gibbon Fiberglass Reproductions in his home town of Gibbon, Nebraska, Dwight Bond and his products have been in the forefront of the street rod industry. First, it was Model A bodies and parts, and components to make a Model T speedster. Then '32 reproductions and sedan delivery conversion kits. When the Model 40 '33s and '34s started coming on, Gibbon was there with the componentry to build a roadster or phaeton. And when the gas crunch hit, they came up with a "compact" '34, the Model Y.

More recently, interest in fat fendered cars led Gibbon Fiberglass to develop its '37 and '39 convertible replicas. To be truthful, Dwight could hardly wait until fat fenders came back into style, because he had rodded and customized a '39 coupe back in his high school years. He still has it and, in fact, used the nerf bar bumpers and '57 Corvette taillights from it in building his personal version of the Gibbon fiberglass rumble seat convertible.

Whether customized or finished "gennie" style with teardrop taillights and original or repro trim, bumpers and appointments, the '39 kit buyer gets the 3-inch chopped windshield, rumble seat and a removeable fiberglass top to be fabric covered and finished Carson style. For this one, Jim McFall (McFall Upholstery in Iowa City, Iowa) used an off-white fabric for an early style appearance and to contrast with the Plum Poly Deltron paint, sprayed by Bill Trumpkey. The convertible also uses a '40 Standard grille and '40 headlights.

Dwight mated a Cordoba torsion bar front suspension to the '39 Frame with one of his company's adaptation kits. A Nova rearend, stock 327 Chevy engine and TH400 automatic transmission are mounted using Chassis Engineering components. Rolling stock consists of Michelin radials on Chevy Ralley wheels with trim rings and hubcaps. George Packard finished off the

engine with a Carter AFB, dual exhausts and modest chrome dress-up goodies.

McFall's stitching over a '67 Toronado power seat, rear jump seat, rumble seat, doors and interior panels is done in tan Naugahyde. A Cadillac tilt-tele steering column is topped with a Banjo Man wheel. A Gennie Shifter, '78 Nova gauges in the fiberglass '40 dashboard, heat and air conditioning, cruise control and a power-controlled rumble seat complete the package.

Now Dwight's daughter can be just like Dad — driving a customized '39 Ford to high school.

From any angle, the '39 Ford convertible is a good looking car, and this customized fiberglass replica, built by Dwight Bond, is no exception. It rides on Michelin radials that surround Chevy Ralley wheels with trim rings and hubcaps.

Removable fabric-covered fiberglass Carson top was finished by McFall Upholstery in Iowa City, Iowa. It features an off-white fabric for an early appearance, and for contrast with Plum Poly paint.

Front seats fold all the way forward to allow access to the rear jump seat. All interior upholstery (and rumble seat) was done by McFall in a tan Naugahyde.

Atop that long deck is a power-controlled rumble seat, for a bit of high-tech nostalgia. Nerf bar bumper and '57 Corvette taillights came from Dwight's original '39 coupe that he drove during his high school days.

A set of '67 Olds Toronado power front seats give driver and passenger comfort for the long cruise. A Cadillac tilt-tele steering column is topped with a Banjo Man wheel. Nova gauges are housed in the glass dash.

A stock Chevy 327 V8 engine and TH400 automatic transmission move the '39 convert down the highway. Engine/trans swap was accomplished using Chassis Engineering components.

GO-FAST FORTY

by Rich Johnson
Vehicle: 1940 Ford Coupe - Pro Street
Owner: David J. Winter — Centerville, Utah

There is never a dull moment in hot rodding. New things are always showing up on the street, often in emulation of what's happening at the races. Years ago, legitimate modifications made for improved dry lakes racing started showing up on the street, even though the mods had nothing whatever to do with improved street performance (at least not at legal speeds). Since the birth of drag racing, it's been the same story; whatever is popular at the strip suddenly starts showing up on the street. In the case of the pro street category, monster motors, fat tires and roll cages are often the quick and easy way to make a performance statement — which is the automotive version of a fashion statement. But some folks aren't satisfied with the quick and easy way. Such a one is David J. Winter.

The statement Winter is making here comes through loud and clear. In emulation of a classic drag car, he has taken the nostalgic styling of a '40 Ford and endowed it with an ultimate performance package. But rather than just stuff a big engine and fat tires in an old car, Winter started from the ground up to develop a serious competition car. Credit for most of the actual work goes to Jim Norman of Provo, Utah. As this book goes to press, the car is yet to be finished, but it is far enough along for us to see how things are going to turn out. Fortunately, David took photos of every step along the way, so we can show how to build a go-fast '40 Ford.

The humble beginnings of this car. It came to Winter as an abandoned project that someone else had been working on. It had a worn out, poorly installed Mustang II front end and a light-duty rearend from a 4-cylinder Mustang. Also included were a badly battered firewall and rotted floor pan.

Left-The back portion of the frame was cut off just ahead of the rear wheel wells, and the fat tires were stuffed inside to help determine measurements for necessary modifications. Correct axle width was calculated to be 43-1/2 inches. Ford 9-inch axle came from a '78 Lincoln Versailles with 11-inch disc brakes.

Right-Using heavy-duty jackstands, the body was propped up to help pre-determine the finished vehicle ride height and clearances with the rear tires under the fenders.

Below-Rear fenders are A.I. Industries fiberglass items which are 3 inches wider than stock to accommodate the fat tires, giving the '40 an even wider stance and a more impressive fat fendered look.

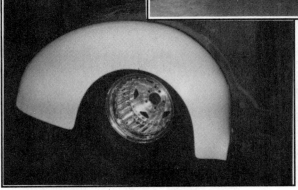

Right-Four-link connects at the rear axle and at a crossmember forward of the wheel well. Adjustable converging angle of links permits the driver to dial in the location of lifting force that occurs during acceleration.

Right-Massive tubs enclose the tires and accentuate how narrow the axle is. Diagonal link serves to locate the axle side-to-side under the chassis.

Lower right-Blocks of wood are used on top of the tires to maintain clearance to the fender well while building the rest of the rear suspension system. All items to assemble the rear suspension were hand built with the exception of the coilover shocks.

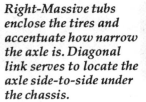

Above-New rear frame members were made from .095" 2"x3" rectangular steel tubing, with tubular crossmembers for strength.

A new firewall was fabricated and installed, properly contoured to accept a big block Chevy engine and TH400 automatic transmission. New Mustang II front suspension system is in place.

Center section of the frame was fabricated of tubular steel, and a transmission mount is ready for a TH400 automatic to be installed behind the big block.

A front driveline loop was built into the center section of the frame.

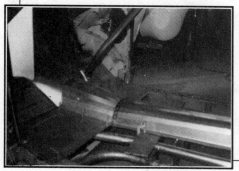

In finest pro street style, a roll cage is an integral part of the car. Cage is made of .095" 1-3/4" tubing. These photos

show the intermediate mounting points for the cage just behind the driver's seat, as well as the rear mounting points behind the wheel tubs.

New Mustang II front suspension is in place, complete with manual rack and pinion steering unit. Stock Mustang II crossmember was later scrapped because it was 2-1/2 inches too wide. New motor mounts later tie in nicely with the hand-built crossmember.

Left-The stock floorpan was a rotted mess, so a new one was fabricated and installed. Note also the front mounting position of the roll cage in the passenger side footwell.

Access hole is for adjusting 4-link and dropping rear coilover shocks for tire changes. When no access is necessary, there is a cover for the hole.

Is there enough rubber under there to suit a pro streeter's dream? Rear tires are 33x21.5x15 on 15x15 Centerline wheels.

Above-At the mid-point of project construction, the car was rolled out into daylight to see how she looked, and maybe to tease the neighborhood boys a little.

Right-With the body off, we get an excellent view of how the chassis is constructed. It was at this point that the discovery was made that the Centerline wheel offset didn't work with the stock Mustang crossmember and wouldn't allow complete turns.

Right-Notice that each mounting point of the roll cage is directly connected to the frame, rather than just attaching to the floorboard of the car. The front bar bends slightly and attaches to the mounting point in the passenger side footwell.

Right-Front section of frame rails were fully boxed, and a custom-built crossmember installed, along with a new strut rod and mount.

Rear roll cage mounts are braced to the frame. In this photo we see the first glimpse of how the coilover shocks were installed between the axle housing and a tubular cross-member in the frame kickup section.

Battery box fits up between the wheel tubs, just forward of the rear axle. Note the cover over the access hole for adjusting the 4-link and coilover shocks.

Seat boxes are installed for driver and passenger. Tabs for racing seat belts are included. Hyster forklift seat adjuster is cheap and adaptable to racing seats.

A new hood for the go-fast '40 came from Wescott. Note here the substructure for the fiberglass hood.

Front fenders are Wescott items, and the grille and vent sides were pieced together.

The finished floorpan, looking at it the easy way, shows how everything went together and where the weld seams are. From a rusted pile of scrap iron, this car is starting to take shape.

From this view of the rear axle, it's easy to see how the 4-link and track locater are positioned. Note bracing across the back of and beneath the Ford 9-inch axle housing.

A Honda cable trunk release on a new bracket has been tacked in place for trial fit. The new rear body panel has not yet been installed, as can be seen by the corrosion in the old panel.

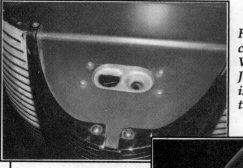

Hood latch and safety catch are out of a Volkswagen Rabbit or Jetta donor car. Release is by cable from inside the car.

The foamed fuel cell will be installed in this area between and to the rear of the wheel tubs. Note the support basket for the fuel cell down between the frame rails.

To the rear of the grille pan is the radiator cover, which bolts to the grille pan through the recessed hole in each end. This cover and the grille pan will later be chromed.

Steering connections are made at the end of the column, again just above the heim locater, and then at the rack and pinion unit shaft. Note the strut rod bracket below the frame rail.

A hand-built steering column and below-dash mounting bracket are poised and ready to have the dashboard reinstalled.

This angle shows how the roll cage goes together above the driver's and passenger's heads. Entire cage can be removed or replaced with the body on and the interior intact. Steering wheel features a push button release.

Bronze-bushed hidden hinges are equipped with grease fittings. Hinges are constructed on a simple jig to ensure accurate alignment of pin shafts.

Right-When the car was ready to have the doors installed, the hidden hinges tucked nicely into their recesses. Here is the driver's side upper hinge after installation.

Additional bracing was installed for the roll cage, as well as for mounting positions for the racing seat belts. This much attention to the details of a roll cage is seen only in serious competition cars.

DELUXE FORTY

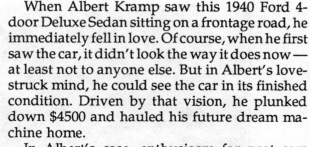

by Rich Johnson   photos by James Handy

1940 Ford 4-Door Deluxe Sedan
Owner: Albert Kramp — Stockton, California

When Albert Kramp saw this 1940 Ford 4-door Deluxe Sedan sitting on a frontage road, he immediately fell in love. Of course, when he first saw the car, it didn't look the way it does now — at least not to anyone else. But in Albert's love-struck mind, he could see the car in its finished condition. Driven by that vision, he plunked down $4500 and hauled his future dream machine home.

In Albert's case, enthusiasm for neat cars didn't just suddenly spring forth and take control of his life. It's been a twenty-year affair of the heart that began as innocent admiration for other peoples' cars. Then it led through a trail of personal car ownership including a '50 Chevy, a '61 Corvette and a '23 bucket "T".

Because of limits on Albert's time to work on the car himself, (making a living often gets in the way of doing really important stuff, like building a hot rod), when it came time to convert fantasy into reality, Albert sought the expertise of Ellsworth Hein Street Rods to oversee the project.

The powertrain consists of a '76 Chevy 350 V-8 engine that was bored .030" and topped by an Offenhauser manifold and Holley carburetor. Chromed 2-inch exhaust headers are by TCI, with turbo mufflers down the line. A '74 Chevy automatic transmission takes care of gear selection and sends the torque to the 3.08:1 differential.

Front suspension was borrowed from a Mustang II, and the rear came out of a Chevy II. Chromed coil springs soften the bumps front and rear. In order to match bolt patterns front and rear, a set of '73 Chevy front disc brakes were installed. The steering box is Mustang, and the column came from a GM van.

One complication during the completion of the car was locating an upholsterer to do the car the way Albert wanted it done. To solve the dilemma, he opened his own shop under the name Al Kramp Specialties and hired master upholsterer Joe Holcomb to do the work. Part of the interior work was filling the dash and installing a set of gauges from Classic Instruments.

Don Perry did the bright red paint job, using acrylic lacquer. With all the brightwork installed and the glass tinted, this Deluxe Forty is a stunning sight goin' down the road — as all REAL rods are prone to do.

A '76 Chevy 350 V8 was bored .030" over and equipped with an Offenhauser manifold and Holley carb. Chromed 2" exhaust headers and turbo mufflers take care of the exhaust.

In case you happen to bend down for an under-belly inspection, there are chromed coil springs on the Chevy II rearend to greet the eye.

Classic Instruments fill the dashboard, and the driver is treated to the soft grip of an engraved LeCarra wheel. Note the air conditioner vents peeking out from beneath the dash.

The tilt steering column was donated by a GM van. Finding an upholsterer to do the car the way Albert wanted was a problem, so he opened his own upholstery shop to take care of it.

Upholstery was carried over into the trunk, giving the car a nicely completed appearance.

PRO STREET '40

Fat fenders, fat tires and fat engine

by Rich Johnson

Vehicle: 1940 Ford Sedan
Owners: Tom and Linda Durocher
Union Lake, Michigan

Here's the problem: Social responsibility is not evenly distributed among the masses. Some folks are forced to carry more than their fair share of the burden, simply because of the kind of business they are in. Such a pity! An example is Tom Durocher, owner of Thomas' Street Rods in Pontiac, Michigan. Because of his business, Tom is expected to drive something special. Can't be something plain, simple and lately from down the road in Detroit. Gotta be something neat.

So, in loyal fulfillment of his public responsibility, Tom decided to build a little something that would uphold his position as a leader in the local street rod industry. Just a little pro street '40 Ford sedan with some color and zip. A touch of B&M Mega Blower here, a couple of Holley 600 carbs there, a dash of balanced and blueprinted 350 Chevy engine for spice. All in the line of duty, you understand.

Actually, we are not fully convinced that Tom and Linda have done all this purely as a means of shouldering the burden of public responsibility. We suspect that the Durochers secretly grin and chuckle to themselves as they motor along Michigan highways, flaunting their fat fenders, fat tires, and fat motor. They aren't feeling any duty-related pressure. They can't fool us!

We're on to you, Tom and Linda. You guys are enjoying every minute in this car, all the while pretending that you are forced to drive it to uphold your image. Hah!

Actually, we have evidence that the Durochers aren't the only ones who enjoy this machine. Every head swivels enthusiastically as the blown V8 rumbles past, every face breaks into a smile. Every male (and lots of females) with healthy corpuscles begin to salivate and flex their fingers in mock grip of the steering wheel, imagining themselves in the cockpit of such a road rocket. All of this is natural, and no cause for alarm (just in case you find yourself drooling on these pages, and fear that it's time to see the doctor about corrective measures).

If enthusiasm for this pro street '40 seems excessive, take a look at all the neat stuff that's here. The steel body has been cleaned up and modified in all the right places. There is a rolled rear pan and a third brake light with nine LED crystals in the face. Doors were shaved and the hood peaked. A monster Harwood scoop makes room for the monster mouse motor that lives under the hood. Smoothie running boards were installed, and, of course, the rear was tubbed to accommodate fat rubber.

To show off all this custom work, an Easter basket full of colors were chosen from the PPG Deltron palette. Paint work was done by Thomas' Street Rods, and the graphic design was completed by Larry Shovan who is an art and design consultant at Thomas' Street Rods.

While not so colorful, the interior is every bit as beautiful as the exterior. Upholstered in doeskin vinyl, the Lear Sigler bucket seats offer style and comfort for the front seat passengers. Amazingly enough, even though this is a pro street version of the '40 Ford, there is a full-width rear bench seat that was handmade for the car. Clean, is the key word to any description of the high quality workmanship on the inside. VDO instruments are the only interruption to an otherwise completely smooth dashboard. The Kenwood stereo and various electric switches are housed inside the glovebox.

Rear suspension consists of the marriage between elliptical springs, 4-bar, and panhard rod hardware. Up front there is a dropped axle and 4-bar setup. Disc brakes do the stopping, and rear traction is provided by 15x33 Mickey Thompson tires mounted to Centerline aluminum wheels.

To spin all that rubber, some lively ponies were stuffed into the engine compartment. A Chevrolet 350 cid V8 was treated to flat-top pistons and steel crank, then balanced and blueprinted for smooth high-rpm operation. Hand-machined valve covers add a touch of glitter to the engine, while a pair of Holley 600 carburetors atop a B&M Mega Blower add sparkle to the performance. Exhaust is routed through headers to SuperTrapp mufflers which peek out below the running boards. Engine cooling is taken care of by a custom fabricated high efficiency crossflow radiator. Gear selection is the duty of a TH350 automatic transmission that has been improved by B&M.

Yeah, it isn't exactly fair. Some folks have to carry a heavier load of social responsibility than the rest, but Tom and Linda Durocher pull it off pretty well.

This car was purchased in 1989, and started on the road to pro street heaven. It was an old street rod that originally had been built sometime around 1976. It sported all the moldings and the body was still stock.

Everything was stripped from the car, and it was prepared for new goodies in the engine compartment. A dropped axle and 4-bar front suspension was installed, and the car employs Saginaw steering.

At the appropriate moment, the balanced and blueprinted Chevy 350 was dropped between the rails. Equipped with dual Holley 600 carbs and a B&M Mega Blower, this mill will definitely rotate the tires.

Larry Shovan (art and design consultant at Thomas' Street Rods) did the graphics and paint work. Here he is at work, with a fairly detailed picture of the graphics concept for the car taped on the door as inspiration and to serve as a guide.

Upholstered in doeskin vinyl, the Lear Sigler bucket seats offer style and comfort for front seat passengers. VDO instruments grace a completely smooth dashboard. A Kenwood sound system and various electric switches are hidden inside the glovebox.

FAT
BUNCH '41

by Rich Johnson   photos by James Handy

Vehicle: 1941 Ford Pickup
Owner: Bob Miller — Yuba City, California

Relatively stock body is beautiful despite the fact that it wasn't even chopped, channeled, sectioned or reworked in any way. It has a classic styling that is just fine the way it came from the factory.

Bob Miller is a fat kinda guy. No, we don't mean it *that* way! It's just that he is the type of fellow who likes fat fendered stuff well enough to join a club named the Fat Bunch. At age 50+, Bob has been involved in the love of street rods since the early '50s. A list of his previous rides is revealing. In addition to a few other cars, he has owned three '41 Ford coupes, and a '46 convertible. See what we mean about Bob being a fat kinda guy?

Originally, Bob bought this '41 pickup for $400. Then he spent some 15 years building it into what we see here. Power comes from a '47 Ford flathead that was bored .060" over, yielding a total displacement of 255+ cubic inches. The heads were polished and the block relieved, then an Isky 3/4 cam was installed and the valvetrain was upgraded to Johnson adjustable solid lifters. Isky springs close the valves tightly each cycle. An Eddie Meyer Hollywood intake manifold has been topped with a pair of Stromberg 97 carbs. Exhaust is routed by way of a set of Fenton headers, through turbo mufflers.

Gear selection is the duty of a 1977 T-10 4-speed transmission that has been upfitted with altered stock shift linkage. The final member of the drivetrain is a '57 Ford station wagon 9-inch rear axle, stuffed with 3.56:1 gears. Spring packs for both the stock '41 front axle and the rear unit have been treated to Teflon between the leaves.

Steering, from wheel to box, is totally stock '41 Ford, except that the column was chromed. But the brakes have undergone some updating. Front binders are '73 Chevy discs, and the rear units are '57 Ford drums. TruSpoke wheels (14x7 front, 15x8 rear) are wrapped with Armstrong radials (215/70R14 front, 235/70R15 rear).

Body and frame are basically stock, but somehow everything looks better than Ford ever intended back in '41. Of course, it helps to have a bunch of chrome under the hood, the engine painted red, the chassis painted black, and endless-depth of red lacquer paint everywhere else. A hand-rubbed oak cargo bed adds a distinct touch of class. Then there's the button-tufted white Naugahyde interior, complete with fuzzy white dice hanging from the rearview mirror. It looks dynamite! The stock dash has been fitted with King Seely 12-volt instruments, and a Sears sound system was installed.

Along the way, a number of custom parts had

to be made and creative installation performed. Among them were the triangulated 4-bar rear, alternator and air conditioner brackets, placement of the air outlets, controls and evaporator, as well as the radio beneath the seat.

Besides the pure enjoyment Bob gets from driving this piece of automotive artwork, he has garnered a stack of awards from numerous shows. Friends Ben Collins and Mike Overton can also take pride in the workmanship. Ben rebuilt the crossmember and put in the T-10 4-speed, using an Offy adapter, split the wishbone and built a new floorpan. Mike helped out with making the rearend fit, fabricated all-aluminum pulleys, air cleaner, and did the aluminum and stainless welding.

It's good to have friends like this when you're a fat kinda guy.

Although the truck looks low, it is riding on stock front and rear leaf springs, which have been treated to Teflon between each leaf. Tires are 215x14 in front and 235x15 in the rear, stuffing the wheelwells full of rubber.

Classic flathead styling, with enough chrome and polish to encourage the use of sunglasses. The '47 Ford V8 was bored .060" over, stacked with an Eddie Meyer Hollywood intake manifold and topped with a pair of Stromberg 97s. Fenton headers route the exhaust.

Hand-rubbed oak cargo bed adds a touch of class. It's things like this that bring home the trophies from area shows.

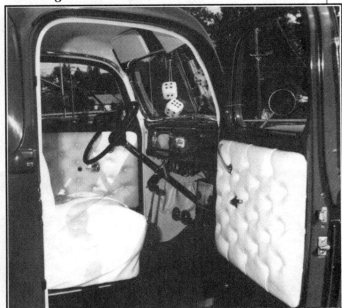

Button-tufted white Naugahyde upholstery brightens up the interior in Fifties style. Fuzzy dice are the crowning touch.

HOT PINK '47

by Rich Johnson

Vehicle: 1947 Ford Coupe
Owners: Dave and Judy Deitz — Bakersfield, California

In seven months time, this '47 coupe went from parts and pieces to a hot pink fat rod worthy of dreams. Working from 4 to 8 o'clock in the morning, and weekends, Dave and Judy rolled this one out in record time.

Real hot rodders don't sleep all the way through the night like normal people, wasting time on idle dreams. Nah, they'd rather spend the wee hours in the shop working on the real thing — building the kind of car that dreams are made of. At least that's they way Dave and Judy Deitz do it.

Dave and Judy are owners of Valley Rigs 'N Rods in Bakersfield, California. By day, they run the shop. By night, they built what we see on these pages. This '47 Ford coupe was constructed in a total of 7 months, working from 4 to 8 o'clock in the morning each day. Then the shop doors opened for normal business. Saturdays and Sundays, Dave would sneak down to the shop and spend the whole day building on the coupe. That's the kind of thing you do when you're a real hot rodder.

Hot Pink is our name for this car, not Dave and Judy's, and we call it that for a couple of reasons. Pink is actually the color of the car, and this is one HOT automobile, in terms of performance. A monster 468 cubic inch, balanced and blueprinted Chevy motor has found a home under the hood, and a bunch of neat stuff has been done to perk up the big block. A 280 Magnum cam plays the tunes that keep the roller rockers dancing. Forged pistons have been dressed in moly rings, and are driven by a polished and drilled crankshaft. A Pete Jackson gear drive makes sure timing is accurate for the Accel distributor, fired by a MSD 6A capacitive discharge ignition system. Fuel is fed by a 427 hi-po fuel pump through a 750 Edelbrock carburetor which is poised atop a Performer intake manifold. And if gasoline isn't quite enough for the occasion, there is the nitrous oxide system to wake the engine up.

Following the engine is a TH400 automatic transmission that has been treated to a shift kit and a 2300 rpm stall converter, all built by A-1 transmission. Torque is transmitted to a Lincoln Versailles rearend, with 3.25:1 axle ratio.

The Lincoln rearend is kind of a trick piece because it has stock disc brakes with a built-in parking brake system. In the front is a Mustang II front end with a Heidt crossmember, Heidt dropped spindles, Ford Granada rotors and GM calipers. E.C.I. provided the Corvette 4-

wheel disc brake master cylinder and power booster.

A stock Ford frame was used as the beginning point for the modified chassis that finally became the foundation for this hot '47 coupe. Wheels are solids, with Ford hubcaps and trim rings. Tires are 255-60x15 in the rear and 205-75x14 up front.

The body is completely steel, and Dave did all the body and paint work himself. He even built the engine, but had machine work performed by Sam's Auto Parts.

Looking over the photos, it is safe to say that this is just the kind of fat Ford that would be worth getting up in the middle of the night to work on. Dave and Judy have proved the point.

The old firewall was removed and a new one made up out of 10-gauge sheetmetal, and was set back 2-1/2 inches to increase clearance for the big block. The car retained the stock floorboard.

Awaiting installation, the balanced and blueprinted 468 cid Chevy sports a 280 Magnum cam, roller rockers, Pete Jackson gear drive, Edelbrock Performer manifold (to be topped by a 750 carburetor), forged pistons with moly rings, and a polished and drilled crank.

Center X-member (passenger side) before modification, and driver's side after the new rail has been installed. A Heidt's crossmember has been installed (foreground) to accommodate a Mustang II front suspension.

Here, the center crossmember has been removed entirely, and the new rails installed on both sides. This opens up the space required for the TH400 automatic transmission. The rear crossmember will come out and be replaced with 2-inch square tubing.

Lincoln Versailles rearend has been slipped into place. This rearend features disc brakes with an integral parking brake system. Square tubing was installed for gas tank and upper shock mount support.

Corvette master cylinder and power booster are 4-wheel disc brake units from E.C.I. Here they are installed and plumbed.

Mustang II front suspension is in place, and the engine has found its home. Heidt's dropped spindles have yet to be installed. The car will get Ford Granada rotors and GM calipers from E.C.I.

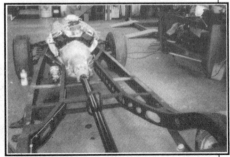

The center X-member has been completed, and a driveshaft loop built in as part of the rear crossmember. The engine was fired and tested before the body was installed, using a 55-gallon drum of water for coolant during the test.

Finally, the body was set on the chassis and made ready for bodywork and paint. Body remained mostly stock, with only a few subtle custom modifications.

Driver's side is just about finished. The rear fender was installed to check clearance over the tire. With replacement rear axle width measured against stock axle before starting project, there should be no clearance problems at this point.

Because the car is going to be a daily driver, Dave applied rubberized undercoating on the underside of the body and on the frame to protect against rock chips and to deaden road noise. It is easy to hose off, and looks like new when dry.

Rear bumper has been smoothed and the license plate bracket has been cut in and molded. Taillights were lowered and tunneled into fenders.

Air Tique heat and air conditioning is installed to the firewall. One-inch square tubing was welded to the back of the firewall as a support for the air conditioner unit.

Inner fender panels were cut and widened to accommodate the aluminum crossflow radiator. New radiator support was fabricated out of 1-1/2 inch channel, moved forward 9 inches. Right fender has '73 El Camino gas filler door welded in for radiator fill access. When the hood is closed, it holds the door down.

New radiator support is visible. Stock grille panel is shortened and bent back to meet new front fender wells. New bottom panel will scoop air straight to radiator, and will be made of 10-gauge flatstock. Headlights are spaced back 2-1/2 inches for '56 Ford F-100 headlight rims and stock headlight buckets.

Water pump is behind center of radiator and can run a 19-inch fan without clearance problems, offering plenty of cooling power.

New lower grille panel is going together, scooped to the radiator. Note turn signals in top grille bar.

An aluminum dash insert was custom built and then filled with a complement of VDO Nite Design gauges. Note the air conditioner controls and registers.

Dave says, "The car is only about six months old, so I still have to bottle-feed it." Nitrous oxide bottle is painted to match hot pink exterior color, and looks good tucked in the corner of the upholstered trunk.

A little touch of ground effects ahead of the fender. Can this possibly help the gas mileage?

Windshield was V-butted, glued, and surrounded with an S-10 Chevy windshield rubber. Shaded glass came out of a bus. Pieces were too large, so they needed to be cut. Care was taken to line up equal amounts of shading before cutting.

Front seat is a 60/40 split bench with a fold-down center armrest out of an '82 Oldsmobile Cutlass Supreme. Upholstery material is GM grey velour with '90 Chevy tweed inserts.

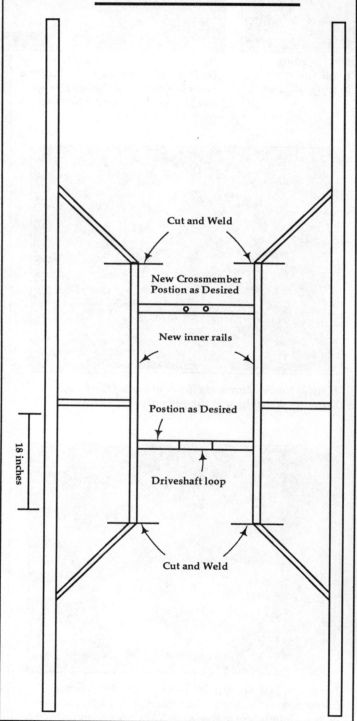

VALLEY RIGS N' RODS
X-MEMBER KIT
FOR '41 - '48 FORD FRAMES

Cut and Weld

New Crossmember
Postion as Desired

New inner rails

Postion as Desired

Driveshaft loop

18 inches

Cut and Weld

The dashboard is padded and covered with grey vinyl, as are all window moldings. Keeps the arms cool when you hang them out the window on a hot day.

An aluminum panel covers the radiator. Access to filler is via door on passenger side fender. Engine compartment is clean, and the monster that lives here makes this Hot Pink rod deserve its name.

LOW FAT FORTY-SEVEN

by Rich Johnson

Vehicle: 1947 Ford Convertible
Owner: Tom Mattern — Ft. Wayne, Indiana

Why Ford didn't make 'em this way to begin with is a mystery. Smooth, low and fat is the obvious choice for discerning car lovers. Black fabric on the chopped soft top looks good with the rest of the exterior treatment.

Fat Fords is what this book is all about, so if your eyeballs are on this page, there is evidence that you believe fat is good — speaking in non-dietary terms, of course. Well, if fat is good, low fat must be even better. And a low fat '47 that looks as sweet as Tom Mattern's is especially nice.

Here is a car that is admired by all who see it. It's sleek and low and smooth and beautiful. Yet there was nothing magic about building it. The car started out as a grungy old drop top Ford that stood too tall and was cluttered with too much factory trim, but it was lucky enough to fall into the right hands.

In this case, the right hands began with Gerry Charvat's Hot Rod Shop in Ft. Wayne, Indiana. Construction took place over a period of 14 months, and the car was ready for the 1990 Street Rod Nats.   At the Hot Rod Shop, the body was stripped from the frame and prepared for new life on a new chassis. The replacement chassis was a '72 Chevelle that had been modified as seen in the chassis section of this book. This kind of chassis swap is becoming ever more popular because it results in a car with classic styling that has excellent ride, handling and braking characteristics.

Of course, you don't end up with a car such as this without a few body modifications. In addition to a list of minor operations, the major body mods include rolled front and rear pans, MoPar headlights that were recessed 1/4 inch, a change in the front fender crease from the old hook shape to a more modern "L" shape, removal of the running boards and extension of the body 1-1/4 inches, rear fender contour change at the bottom to match the rear pan, installation of a recessed van license plate housing, and a fresh set of '80s Mustang sideview mirrors. All the unnecessary trim (including handles) was removed to enhance the smooth body lines. Taillights are '87 Corvette third brake lights, which look just right in the narrow panel below the deck lid.

In order to qualify for the low fat designation, the top was chopped 2-1/2 inches. The full procedure for chopping this convertible top is covered in the Tex Smith book, *How To Chop*

Tops. This (and the chassis swap) brought the car's overall height down to a pleasing level.

1982 Buick Riviera power front seats and console were installed, and the passenger seat is a recliner. The rear seat was custom built to fit. In addition to custom fabric and leather upholstery work performed by Harvey Holman, the interior was treated to a custom-built dashboard by the guys at the Hot Rod Shop. Convenience accessories include air conditioning, power windows, and a tilt steering column, as well as power antenna, doors, deck lid and mirrors. Glass has been tinted 10% grey, and the windshield was V-butted.

Under the hood is a 396 cid Chevy V8 that has been built with a .030" overbore. A TH350 automatic transmission with lock-up torque converter is in charge of gear selection, and torque is transmitted to a set of BFGoodrich tires on Centerline wheels.

Rob Butler, of Ft. Wayne, Indiana, was delegated responsibility for all the paint work. He employed a combination of special mix purple, blue and magenta, in addition to Ford gray. With the black soft top up or down, this is one dynamite looking car.

Nobody can argue — low fat is the way to go.

In the beginning, there was nothing but a grungy old drop top Ford that was awaiting some creative care. Fourteen months later, the finished car was ready for the Nats.

A chassis swap was in order, and a '72 Chevelle chassis was modified to fit beneath the fat Ford body. Modification of this chassis is covered in this book in the section about chassis.

The floor received a bit of modification in the area of the trunk and rear seat, to accommodate the late GM frame. The spare tire well was removed and a piece of flat sheetmetal installed. Below the rear seat, the floor was contoured to fit the frame kickup. Later on, the entire undercarriage was detailed in show-car style.

With the fat Ford body mounted to the late GM chassis, there is a neat marriage between classic styling and modern ride, handling and braking characteristics.

Rear coil springs and shock absorbers from the late GM chassis give the car a comfortable ride. Just ahead of the fender opening, you can see where the running boards were removed and the lower body panel extended 1-1/4 inches.

With the body pretty much together, the running board removal
and lower body panel extension is
clearly visible. Handles and trim
have been removed, and the rear
pan rolled.

Front pan has been rolled and
MoPar headlights installed with a
1/4-inch recess. Note the way the
body accent crease in the front
fender has been changed from a
hook shape to an "L" shape.

Part of the custom interior work
performed by the Hot Rod Shop
was the dashboard. After fabrication, the dash was installed and
filled with all the right gauges.

Front seats are from an '82 Buick
Riviera, and the rear bench was
custom built to fit. Leather and fabric
upholstery work was performed by
Harvey Holman of Ligonier, Indiana.

To bring the top down 2-1/2 inches, the windshield was cut and then the top mechanism was lowered straight
down. No modifications are necessary to the top bows, only to the side irons to compensate for the way the top
changes length as it is lowered. For detailed coverage of this top chop, see Tex Smith's book How To Chop Tops.

Left-Enough horses for the highway
come from a built Chevy 396 V8.
Behind that is a TH350 automatic
transmission with lock-up torque
converter.

Right-A pair of '87 Corvette third brake
lights serve as taillights for the low fat
Ford, fitting elegantly in the body panel
beneath the deck lid. Recessed license
plate housing was borrowed from a
van. Now is this car sleek, or what!

193

DROP TOP '48

by John Lee

Vehicle: 1948 Ford Convertible
Owner: Dennis McClure — Broomfield, Colorado

Speedway 4-inch dropped I-beam front suspension has been equipped with TCI shock mounts, reverse spring eyes and sway bar. Modifications lowered the sheetmetal to near ground level, for a just right stance.

In the 27 years since he got his first driver's license, Dennis McClure has seen several street rods come and go, not to mention a variety of other cars. But of them all, the late '40s Fords are his favorites. As each one departed, it left thoughts in his mind of how the next one could be an improvement over the last.

When the sedan was sold, the next rod was to be a coupe. After the coupe left…well, you know how it goes. Dennis finally arrived at the point where he could afford the time and the funds to build his ultimate '46-'48 model. This '48 convertible represents that goal.

Starting with a complete car that had been restored years earlier, Dennis turned it over to Dan Kittelman at DK Carriage Works in Lafayette, Colorado with instructions to "make it smooth." That includes the frame which, once the body was removed, was boxed and all unneeded holes filled. Stainless trim was removed from the hood, deck and fenders, and longer strips installed on the doors to cover the holes left by removal of the handles. Both hood and deck lid were punched with louvers, the latter requiring separating the skin from the frame structure, then putting it back together after the holes were punched.

The top grille bar was frenched. Taillights were swapped side for side and set in a lower position on the fenders. Both front and rear bumpers were sectioned six inches and the bolt holes filled. Kittelman finished his work in GM Carmine urethane, then had Stan's Signs add red pinstriping.

Before again being mated to the customized body, the chassis was prepared for its new life by Gary Vahling and crew at Masterpiece Rodding. A 4-bolt 350 cid Chevy short block was fitted out with a Delorto dual two-barrel manifold and carbs, Chevy HEI ignition, and hugger headers flowing into turbo mufflers. A Walker radiator and ACS thermostatically controlled electric fan handle the cooling. A filled firewall, stainless steel lines, Allen head screws and tasteful use of chrome accessories result in a bright, neat engine compartment.

Dennis controls the power application through a 10-inch Chevy clutch and Muncie 4-speed with a Hurst shifter. A Nova 10-bolt rear with 3.57:1 gears was installed with a Chassis Engineering kit, with three-inch blocks and the removal of one spring leaf providing lowering.

Setting the front low around the Real Wheels is a Speedway I-beam with a 4-inch drop, fitted with Magnum disc brakes and Monroe tube shocks on TCI mounts. Steering gear is Chevy, hooked to an IDIDIT aluminum tilt column and LeCarra wheel.

Ron Nelson at Auto Weave did the honors on the interior with gray leather upholstery and dark gray wool carpeting. The rear seat is stock, while the front buckets derive from a Datsun 510. Stewart Warner instruments are housed in a handbuilt aluminum panel. The option list includes an Audiovox stereo system, power windows and ACS heat and air conditioning system.

Henry Ford wanted each of his products to be better than the last one, but he kept changing the styles. Dennis McClure shows what might have resulted if Ford had continued to develop his first post-war series.

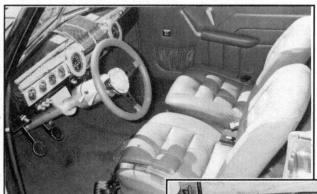

Stewart Warner instruments keep track of vital signs, and an IDIDIT aluminum steering column has been topped with a LeCarra wheel. Accessories include Audiovox stereo system, power windows and air conditioning.

Front bucket seats are Datsun 510 items, while the rear bench is a stock unit. Grey leather upholstery was stitched up by Auto Weave, and dark grey wool carpeting covers the floor.

Vaughn Real Wheels are wrapped with BFGoodrich T/A radials. Tire size in the back is 235x15 while fronts are 185x14.

Taillights were reversed side for side and then lowered 6 inches. Rear bumper was sectioned and filled, then the deck lid was louvered and shaved.

A 4-bolt Chevy 350 runs Delorto dual 2-barrel manifold, HEI ignition and hugger headers. Walker provided the radiator, and cooling is helped by a thermostatically controlled electric fan. Chrome and stainless tastefully dress up the engine compartment.

WILD SIDE

by Gene Winfield

Vehicle: 1948 Ford Coupe
Owner: Pete Marriott — Lake Orion, Michigan

We were at a rod run when a rump-rump from a most healthy motor interrupted our concentration. Looking up, we couldn't see what was making all the commotion, because it was something lower than our RV window. It turned out to be a radically altered 1948 Ford coupe called "On The Wild Side," and wild it certainly is. Owner Pete Marriott of Lake Orion, Michigan went all the way with the custom hot rod treatment on this one.

The 1946 Ford frame has been boxed and fitted with an AMC front suspension, mated to Chevy spindles and disc brakes. Steering is via power rack and pinion. Rear suspension is a '70 Chevelle axle assembly with coil springs.

Body modifications include a 5-1/2" top chop, and all the alterations necessary to convert the roof to a hardtop style. The roof was shortened, and the rear window made flush. That much top chop would be expected to make the car low, but it's even lower because the body was sectioned 5 inches. The car is so low that the 468 cubic inch Chevrolet with 6-71 GMC blower sticks through the hood, so there ain't nobody foolish enough to think this is a no-go show rod.

Headlights were widened 1-1/2 inches and frenched into the raised/radiused/sectioned/molded fenders. Rear fenders got the same treatment. The doors have rounded corners, and the bottoms made into the rockers. Sectioning the hood 4 inches complements the nosed and molded treatment. The trunk was also sectioned 4 inches. The grille bar is made from a 1955 Chrysler bumper guard which has been narrowed and had turn signals added, while the rear bumper is a 1955 Chrysler bumper guard that has been narrowed and frenched with taillights and turn signals installed.

All the body and paint work was done by Pete. The custom mix pearl purple lacquer with clear coat features pin striping by Harry Harding of Clarkston, Michigan. Bob Fender of Clarkston did up the interior in stunning red and grey. The dash is a filled and narrowed 1954 Ford item, and the seats are narrowed Chevy pieces.

Now, what did we forget? Oh yes, the hubcaps are 1957 Cads with spinners (for the custom crowd), and the cam is a Chevy solid with .620" lift (for the rodders). On the wild side? Man, that's an understatement of mammoth proportions!

With a 5-1/2" top chop and a 5" section job, this car has taken a low and slinky custom stance. Grille is '55 Chrysler bumper guard that has been narrowed and had turn signals added.

The dashboard is a filled and narrowed '54 Ford item, and the seats are narrowed Chevrolet units. Note the rear quarter glass that has been shaped to fit the custom hardtop style of this roof.

All show and no go? No way! This 468 cid V8 Chevrolet with 6-71 GMC blower and 3 Holley 2-barrel carbs. Headers are split for four separate exhaust systems.

From the rear, this sleek '48 Ford exudes the feeling of a fat fendered car of the period. Round and low is the key.

Rear bumper is actually the bumper guard from a '55 Chrysler that has been narrowed and frenched with taillights and turn signals added.

Sources

A-1 Racing Parts
770 Route 28
Middlesex, NJ 08846
(201) 968-2323

A.I. Fiberglass
6599 Washington Blvd.
Elkridge, MD 21227
(301) 796-4382

Air Tique
915 N. Nolan River Rd.
Cleburne, TX 76031
(817) 641-6933

Aldan Shocks
646 E. 219th St.
Carson, CA 90745
(213) 834-7478

Automotive Specialties
1050 Columbia Ave.
Sunnyside, WA 98944
(509) 837-3778

Bitchin' Products
9392 Bond Ave.
El Cajon, CA 92021
(619) 449-2837

Bob's Classic Auto Glass
430 Morrill Ave.
Reno, NV 89512
(702) 322-8887

Bob Drake Reproductions
1899 NW Hawthorne Blvd.
Grants Pass, OR 97526
(503) 474-0043

Borgeson
1050 S. Main St.
Torrington, CT 06790
(203) 482-8283

Bradley Antique Auto
4200 S. Interstate 85
Charlotte, NC 28214
(704) 392-3206

Buckeye Rubber Parts
4808 Pierpoint Dr.
Dayton, OH 45426
(513) 837-5433

Bumpers by Briz
8002 NE Highway 99, #99
Vancouver, WA 98665
(206) 573-8628

Butch's Rod Shop
2853 North Lawn Ave.
Dayton, OH 45439
(513) 298-2665

Carolina Custom Machine
Rt. 3 Box 376
Clinton, NC 28328
(919) 564-6123

Centech
Box 139 Rt. 2
Pekiomenville, PA 18074
(215) 287-6707

Chassis Engineering
119 N. 2nd St.
West Branch, IA 53358
(319) 643-2645

Chubby Chassis
275 S. "G" St.
San Bernardino, CA 92410
(714) 884-3132

Classic Chassis
PO Box 53
Glenview, IL 60025
(312) 724-7033

Classic Instruments
1678 P Bevercreek Rd.
Oregon City, OR 97045
(503) 655-3520

Dakota Digital
11301 Kuhle Dr.
Souix Falls, SD 57107
(605) 332-6513

Dennis Carpenter Reproductions
Box 26398
Charlotte, NC 28213
(704) 786-8139

Dr. K's Wiring
No. 11 Lakefront Ave.
Gadsden, AL 35904
(205) 543-7165

ECI
PO Box 2361
Vernon, CT 06066
(203) 872-7046

Enos Custom
840 A Capitolio Way
San Luis Obispo, CA 93410
(805) 544-8503

Fairlane Co.
210 E. Walker St.
St. Johns, MI 48879
(517) 224-6460

**Fat Fendered Street
Rod Shop**
13664 Whittram
Fontana, CA 92335
(714) 357-2700

Fat Man Fabrications
8621-C Fairview Rd. Hwy 218
Charlotte, NC 28227
(704) 545-0369

Gennie Shifter Co.
930 S. Broadmoor Ave.
West Covina, CA 91790
(818) 337-2536

**Gibbon Fiberglass
Reproductions**
Box 490
Gibbon, NE 68840
(308) 468-6178

Hart Enterprises
1475 W. Bullard
Fresno, CA 93711
(209) 435-7109

Headers by Ed
2710 16th Ave. S.
Minneapolis, MN 55407
(612) 729-2802

Heidt's Hot Rod Shop
3100 Swallow Lane
Rolling Meadows, IL 60008
(708) 394-1746

Heinzman Street Rod Shop
Rt. 1 Box 43
Phillips, NE 68865
(402) 886-2275

Hoosier Hoods
2290 Salisbury Rd. S.
Richmond, IN 47374
(317) 962-7924

Independent Chassis
182 Vista Ave.
Winnepeg, Manitoba, Canada
R2M 4Y7
(204) 895-0472

**Independent Suspensions
Inc.**
2234 Lakeside
Wentzville, MO 63385
(314) 327-5389

Innovative Rod Shop
3236 Fitzgerald Rd., Unit E
Rancho Cordova, CA 95742
(916) 635-1025

Joe Smith Automotive
3070 Briar Cliff Rd. N.E.
Atlanta, GA 30329
(404) 634-5157

Johnny's Rod Shop
Rt. 8 Box 530
Mooresville, NC 28115
(704) 483-3300

Kugel Komponents
451 Park Industrial Dr.
La Habra, CA 90631-6172
(213) 691-7006

Lobeck's
7555 Bond St.
Cleveland, OH 44139
(216) 439-8143

Lokar Ltd.
21026 Cantel Pl.
Walnut, CA 91789
(714) 594-2269

LTL Industries
5 Commercial Park Rd.
Mason City, IA 50401
(515) 423-1921

Martz Chassis Engineering
508 E. Pitt St.
Bedford, PA 15522
(814) 623-9501

Mr. 40's
2930 McMillan
San Luis Obispo, CA 93401
(805) 544-1404

Mr. Street Rod
18459 Kranenburg Ave.
Bakersfield, CA 93312
(805) 589-1800

**Obsolete Ford
Parts, Inc.**
6601 S. Shields Blvd.
Oklahoma City, OK 73149
(405) 631-3933

Old Ford Parts
9103 E. Garvey Ave.
Rosemead, CA 91770
(818) 288-2290

Outlaw Performance
Box 550 Rt. 380
Avonmore, PA 15618
(412) 697-4876

Patrick's
Box 648
Casa Grande, AZ 85222
(602) 836-1117

Pete and Jakes
11924 Blue Ridge
Grandview, MO 64030
(816) 761-8000

Poliform
7835 San Andreas Rd.
La Selva Beach, CA 95076
(408) 722-4418

Posies
219 N. Duke St.
Hummelstown, PA 17036
(717) 566-3340

**Progressive
Automotive**
125 W. Rome St.
Baltimore, OH 43105
(614) 862-4696

Racemaster
401 Suffolk Ave.
Brentwood, NY 11717
(516) 273-7040

RB's Obsolete Automotive
7130 Hwy 2
Snohomish, WA 98290
(206) 568-5669

R.H. Jones Co.
439 McGlincey Ln.
Campbell, CA 95008
(408) 377-2560

Rodtin
359-A Trousdale Dr.
Chula Vista, CA 92010
(619) 427-3249

Rootlieb Inc.
Box 1829
Turlock, CA 95381
(209) 632-2203

SAC
1815-C Orange Thorpe Park N.
Anaheim, CA 92801
(714) 680-3373

**Sacramento
Vintage Ford**
4675 Alondra Ln.
Sacramento, CA 95841-4140
(916) 489-3444

Sanderson Headers
202 Ryan Way
S. San Francisco, CA 94080
(415) 583-6617

Specialized Auto Parts
7130 Capitol, Box 9405
Houston, TX 77261
(713) 928-3707

Specialty Power Windows
Rt. 2 Good Wyne Rd.
Forsythe, GA 31029
(912) 994-9248

Speed-O-Motive
12061 E. Slauson Ave.
Santa Fe Springs, CA 90670
(213) 945-2758

Speedway Motors
Box 81906
Lincoln, NE 68501
(402) 474-4411

**Springfield
Street Rods**
2111 West Main St.
Springfield, OH 48504
(513) 323-1932

Street & Performance
Rt. 5 #1 Hot Rod Lane
Mena, AR 71953
(501) 394-5711

TCI Engineering
1416 W. Brooks St.
Ontario, CA 91761
(714) 984-1773

The 40 Fort
5440 Marshall, Unit 3
Arvada, CO 80002
(303) 420-9800

The Wire Works
167 Keystone Rd.
Chester, PA 19013
(215) 485-1937

**Valley Auto
Accessories Manufacturing**
619 25th Ave.
Rock Island, IL 61201
(309) 793-4006

Valley Ford Parts Co.
11610 Vanowen St.
North Hollywood, CA 91605
(818) 982-5303

Valley Rigs & Rods
640 Belle Terrace #4
Bakersfield, CA 93307
(805) 834-7271

Valley Vintage
5960 Valentine Rd., Unit 1A
Ventura, CA 93003
(805) 658-7677

Vintage Air
10305 IH 35 N.
San Antonio, TX 78233
(512) 654-7171

Vintage Friends
1218 Carpenter
Humble, TX 77396
(713) 540-2828

Vintique Inc.
402 W. Chapman Ave., Box 65
Orange, CA 92666
(714) 639-3001

Wabbit's Wood Works, Inc.
Rt. 8 Box 260
Cleveland, TX 77327
(713) 592-1211

**Weedetr Street Rod
Components**
1355 Vista Way
Red Bluff, CA 96080
(916) 527-2040

Wescott's Auto Restyling
19701 SE Hwy 212
Boring, OR 97009
(503) 658-3183

**Winfield's Rod
and Custom**
7256 Eton
Canoga Park, CA 91303
(818) 883-2611

201

TEX SMITH'S
**Hot Rod
LIBRARY**

HOW TO BUILD
FAT
FORDS
1935-1948

By Rich Johnson